Facing Heartbreak

Nicole Dake

Published by Nicole Dake, 2024.

FACING HEARTBREAK

First edition. December 27, 2024.

ISBN: 979-8227679031

Written by Nicole Dake.

Table of Contents

Introduction

When we fall in love, we think it's going to last forever. New love is all about passion and raw emotion. We don't think about the things that will make for a lasting love. We just assume that if we love enough, that is going to sustain us.

The thing is, though, for relationships to last it takes more than love. It takes commitment, compromise and good communication. We need to learn skills to make our relationships stand the test of time. However, many of us lack these skills from our upbringing.

If you had a difficult childhood, or trouble with relationships in the past, you may not have the sense of trust in others that is necessary to make a relationship last. This is something that has to be developed in order for our relationships to last past the honeymoon phase.

This book is full of poems about heartbreak, and watching love change. Sometimes, no matter how much you love someone, you grow apart with time. Your desires and goals change. You may find yourselves longing for different things. When that happens, a lot of heartbreak can ensue.

That is what I have written about here. I have spent the last year in disillusionment as I have been watching the foundations of my relationship shift. When you have built your whole life around someone else, and you watch them changing before your eyes, it can feel like the whole foundation of your life is crumbling.

No matter how much things shift, though, love can still stand the test of time if you put in the effort. Love takes work, just like anything else, and I think that many times we don't realize that. We expect love to be self-sustaining. We don't put in the work to make things last. That's when it falls apart.

But even if you find yourself fighting with your lover, or moving in separate directions, there is always hope as long as both people are committed to making it work.

My partner and I moved overseas together, and I couldn't make being an expat work. It has made holes in our relationship in ways that I never thought possible. However, I still have hope. I feel like there can be a way to fix what is broken if we are willing to try.

I hope that these poems resonate with you, and help you open yourself to love, and the possibility of heartbreak that can ensue.

True North

Photo by Ali Kazal on Unsplash

You were my
true north
you took my hand
and I let you
lead me
From here to there
and back again
all across
the world
I took my cues
my direction
from you
But you led me

astray
Far from home
farther than I
could walk
in a day
The winds got colder our love
not enough
to give me shelter
against oncoming storms
You were my
true north
you led me
to this place
I tried
to call home
But without a friend without a purpose
all I did was flounder while you were free to roam as you please
You lost me
out there somewhere you walked
too far ahead
for me to follow
Your quick steps
never faltering
but my short legs
couldn't keep up
your quick pace
and I fell behind
You didn't look back didn't notice
that I was no longer right beside you
You found your place and I lost mine
So much time
wandering alone trying to find you trying to find home

A place to hang my weary hat
to rest
my aching feet beside the fire
but your hearth has no place
for me now

A Day of Love and Beauty

Photo by JOHN TOWNER on Unsplash

The sun rises on
a beautiful new day
full of beautiful possibilities
full of surprises waiting
Another day of love and beauty
and the joy of a new spring
the opening of my heart
like the unfolding of a flower
New buds on the trees

flowering like new love
and new baby animals sharing the love of spring
Everywhere the world is coming alive again
and so am I
Alive with hope
and new possibilities
hope for what comes
joy in another day
of love and beauty
The smile of my child's face the breath of new spring the wind on my face
Spring rain falls
making the world come alive with beauty and color
and a season coming
to see what it brings
Possibilities waiting
new opportunities coming travel and fun
doors opening
Awake and alive
in a beautiful world
full of so many dreams coming true each day

A Girl and Her Dolls

Image
by danivillar from Pixabay

The girl was alone
in the abyss of time
so she made some little dolls with faces that looked like her own
She played with her dolls in little elaborate houses she told stories
with all of them
Playing make believe
making up stories
elaborate stage plays
that grew bigger
and bigger in their scale taking on a life
of their own
But still
she went to sleep
again each night
hugging the dolls close but they couldn't hug back they couldn't love
her had no life of their own
So she breathed
life into their hearts
made them real
with a will of their own a stage play
on the world stage
She made her creations to be loved
by something new
coming alive
longing for something real besides herself
in the endless
vast emptiness
But the creations
couldn't love her
couldn't see her
couldn't fulfill
her endless longing

A fake compelled will a vision of solitude
a longing older than love and that longing
is all there is
An endless emptiness
the vastness of space
the whispers of solitude on an empty plane
Nothing ever enough
to ease the broken heart the pain of endless aloneness
Wanting something more wanting a respite
wanting to be sure
Why am I here?
Why do I exist?
Why am I alone?
She asks into the vast
silence of endless space and nothing answers back just the echoes
of her own screams
there are no answers
just her own dreams

A Hunger for Love

Photo by Rod Long on Unsplash

We all have a hunger
inside us
a longing for love
a need to belong
a way to feel safe
from the storms of life
We are adrift
on this endless sea
the way before us
shrouded in mist
not knowing where we go
only who goes with us

the crew of our ship
There are people in life
we learn to rely on
people who walk by our side
through the perils and dark to hold our hands
and give us strength
to go ever onward
We long for these people and they are so rare
to find kindred souls
people who really understand us and see beneath the surface
Love is a longing
to really be heard
to really be seen
through the walls
of unseen darkness

A Map with No Names

Image by Ylanite Koppens from Pixabay

"The Wheel of Time turns, and Ages come and pass, leaving memories that become legend. Legend fades to myth, and even myth is long forgotten when the Age that gave it birth comes again. In one Age, called the Third Age by some, an Age yet to come, an Age long past, a wind rose above the great mountainous island of Tremalking. The wind was not the beginning. There are neither beginnings nor endings to the Wheel of Time. But it was a beginning."

— Robert Jordan, The Path of Daggers

It's like staring at a map
with no names scrawled
for the places
one must find

I just stare
at the giant X
that marks the spot
but where?
You can't get to where you're going if you don't know where you are
Beating a path
through the forest
following small paths
perhaps made
by rabbits
but not big enough
for you
Somewhere in the distance
you hear a rooster crow
a scream of civilization
somewhere beyond
Then you wonder
do you really
want to go back
to that world?
The world of humans
all built up
with cities
bridges
roads
and trains
All going somewhere so fast they don't stop to look around trusting
that the train will go round to their destination
always the same every day
the bus route set
as if in stone
But your path is different

your path is unsure
not followed before
by other's footsteps
Do you want to go back?
you ask yourself again
as you hear the rooster crow
There is so much of this world still left untouched by human hands
would you not leave it so?
must everything in time
be conquered?
There is no reason
there is no rhyme
only this unfolding
of the wheel of time
Taking you ever forward
ever onward
towards the horizon
that you know lies somewhere just out of sight beyond
the edge of the wood
How far can you go
on this new path
before you run into
something civilized
Again?

Be Careful What You Wish For

© Flynt | Megapixl.com

Dreams and wishes
float by on the wind
going this way and that
with their own little spin
How do we know
when we cast our
thoughts out like nets
what we will catch
when eventually
we pull them back
from the sea

Full of fish?
or have we caught
only a spare tire
and an old boot?
Scraps thrown out into the ocean
years ago
or gifts
of the sea herself
set adrift on the current
Half-formed thoughts like waves lapping against our small boat
predictable and yet somehow the current draws us deeper in
Spiraling, spinning motion and stillness the rocking of the ebb and flow
of the timeless tides reflecting the inner motion of the mind
Paths not taken
roads not chosen
questions and regrets longing and fear
hope and tears
we look so often
back to where we came to a shore far away and now out of sight
How can we know that the place we left is even still there
at all?
How do we know that we will get
to the other shore
in a boat so small?
With hope we cast
our sails and our nets looking for fish
sailing for dreams
trying to find something still unseen
The edge of the horizon blue in either direction how do we know
where we came from and where we still go
Map and compass in hand the stars at night
to guide our hands

to show us the way
across the vast ocean to the new land
All I have is
fishing metaphors
and I don't know
how to fish
much less
teach someone
else to fish
They say
if you give a man
a fish you feed him
only for a day
that much is true
but is today
all we ever have
and could it be
to give him a fish
is enough
to make a better way?
We go off with dreams and our heads held high when we first start out
but we have been going for a long time now things have changed
we have been long away from home long away from land perhaps grown
weary and longing to see a glimpse of the sand

Beautiful Voices

Photo
by Soundtrap on Unsplash

We all have beautiful voices dying to be heard
above the din
of so many people
yelling into the ethers
Everyone has a message something to share
a unique perspective
a heart that cares
How do we calm the din enough to really listen to each voice individually instead of as a collective cacophony of sound
Do we need to wait our turn speak when spoken to?
How do we listen better to all the voices screaming waiting to be heard
above the sound of sirens
There is so much injustice fear, pain and war
in our world today
Everyone has a story
that is important to be told we all can have an impact if our voices can cut through all the other voices
We are all screaming
at the same time together waiting for our chance for someone to listen
Do we need to stop speaking hear the voices of those most in need
of help and healing
How do we prioritize
their needs above our own how do we bring these voices together into a symphony of voices singing together instead of individual refrains
We need to speak these messages we need to tell our stories and there needs to be someone somewhere out there listening as we pray into the silence of this seemingly endless night
Is there a god somewhere listening to our cries
an angel to save us
from all this misery
we have created
or do we need to find

a way to save ourselves?

Broken Things

We all walk around
with broken pieces inside
hearts and souls
laid bare
that we try to hide
How do you heal
without first admitting
that you are broken?
Sometimes we have to show
a bit of vulnerability
we have to open up again
and face the fear of hurt

in order to be free
of the pain of the past
Sometimes I feel like healing is like taping broken pieces back together
with tiny broken hands a kindergarten art project gone badly wrong
Inside my heart
inside my soul
there is this longing
a need to be whole
But how do I become whole when I don't even know what that used to
feel like?
So long ago
when I was so young
I was already broken
already in pain
before I could speak
or knew my own name
Heartbreak has been
no stranger to me
in fact it is the only
constant companion
I have ever known

Building Your Dreams

Photo by Johannes Plenio on Unsplash

We build our dreams
with fragile hands
always wondering
if you are moving forward
or only sliding back
Are your dreams still
out of reach
somewhere far away
beyond the stars
beyond the sea
Are your dreams
so close you can taste them

smell them
feel them
swirling around you
Do you know what
to do to build them
to breath life
into them
Or do you sit staring
at a blank page and
wondering
Sometimes I feel like
my dreams are close
other days far away
and I don't know
which is the truth
It is a constant
push and pull
it is like my dreams
dance around
circling me
or in an elliptical
close, far, close, far
And I don't know how
to catch those magical moonbeams the stuff that dreams are made of
like spun sugar clouds
they float by me
I don't know how
to catch hold
it's like they slip
through my fingers
I don't know how
to hold onto

the ineffable fabric
Maybe dreams aren't
meant to be held
Maybe you have to dissolve and become cloudlike yourself to be able to swim in their seas you have to become the stuff of dreams yourself
to be able to live among them
How do you dissolve
how do you melt
into that spun sugar stuff like clouds wafting by
How do you find
wings to fly away
like those little clouds
How do you become something else that dreams are made of how do you change yourself
As the dreams circle faster in their strange pattern
how do you learn to move in the pattern yourself
Maybe you don't catch
your dreams at all
maybe
you have to become them

Chasing Love

© Anastasiap83 | Megapixl.com

We spend our lives
chasing after love
without realizing
that chasing love
is like chasing moonbeams
Love isn't something
meant to be held
you just sit
and bask in its beauty
unfolding before you
touching something
inside your soul

Coming alive again
coming awake
to the beauty of life
growing within us
The greatest love
the merging
of two hearts
creates our greatest love our children
They come from
the act of our live
growing from us
reminding us always
of the love
of those two hearts
creating
a new heartbeat
A new life grows
from our hearts
born from us
and yet separate
a new soul
a new self
a reflection
of the love of ourselves
We become mothers
become fathers
more than once
we were lovers
the love of a child
caves our hearts deeper opening our souls
to a deeper purpose
and a sense of meaning

Life begets life
love begets love
We propel ourselves forward on the wings of our love growing and dreaming creating something new something more beautiful than we were alone
We need each other
to survive
to thrive
we help each other grow as we share this love
this life
we shape with our hands with our hearts
Souls running free
into a new land
where dreams are born and faith is needed
to guide these new souls the way they should go
Learning lessons
of what really matters finding new hope
in the eyes of a child
ready to learn
ready to thrive
they are at once
our greatest accomplishment and our greatest teachers
Children teach us
to be the best of ourselves to give more
to love more
to be more kind
to be more patient
We learn as we grow
raising each other
a small hand
reaching up
to hold a larger one

together we thrive
together we live
finding new meaning
in a new kind of love

Complain

Photo
by Abigail Keenan on Unsplash

Sometimes I just want
to complain and
throw these thoughts away write them all out then
crumple them up
into a little ball
to be thrown away
Unhappy thoughts for
an unhappy morning
and usually I have a smile but today I have a frown
I need to learn how to stop all of this ranting
and turn this frown
upside down
Time to smile
Time to pretend
everything is fine
and it just takes
a little more time
to get where
I want to be
I had this dream
of sitting on the beach
with my laptop like
some Instagram influencer with the sun in my hair
and the sand in my toes
But life isn't like that
and here I sit
in the rain and the cold

Constant Regret

When you are a mother forced to choose between your children you always choose wrong
There is no right choice
no 'good child'
no 'bad child'
They are all bright
beautiful children
The choice that was wrong was allowing them
to live in separate places separate homes
somewhere far
away from your own
No matter which one
you go to
you leave
the other behind
Our children are our hearts living outside our bodies and mine is ripped in half
One here
one there
Coming home to one
should be a joy
but I leave the other
far behind
and I cry for her
Here or there
stay or go
it is never right
Like a tug of war
with me in the middle
Constant regrets
constant pain
constant shame

that I let it come to this
The one choice
that can't be unmade to let my children separate

Darkness is Coming

© Chepko | Megapixl.com

My tearstained face
looks back from the mirror
I wipe at my eyes
to try to see clearer
the meaning of dreams
just below the surface
a whisper of magic
and a hint of madness
How do we go back
to who we once were
erase the regrets
and become again pure

Our hearts are scarred
from the lies that we told
something shattered inside
something real we can hold
I want to go back
before it began
take back all the wrongs to be free and wild
Let go of the shame fueled by hate and fear try to be something else as the end is draws near
Can we weather
one more storm
in this together
can we walk
again through the fire the endless night
is coming closer
and closer still
Can we fight it back and make things better can we find hope peace and redemption?
Can we erase
the sins of the past do the right thing
and go home at last

Death by a Thousand Cuts

Image by Sandra from Pixabay

Death by a thousand tiny cuts
the pain of knowing I am never enough
Every time you tell me you don't love me
it cuts a little deeper into my mind

into my heart
into my flesh
I am broken
battered and bleeding broken bones mend
but it's never the same you heal a little
but you still limp
on that bad ankle
They lie and tell you the first cut is the deepest but it isn't
it's just a scratch
drawn by frightened hands that don't know how to start to cut
to rend the flesh
to leave a scar
The first time you cut isn't the time you die the first time you bleed you regret
and you tape it up
After a while you forget what life was like
before the pain
hollowing out your soul dying even in dreams you can never be whole

Early Morning Stillness

Photo owned by Author

I wake in the stillness
of the early morning
soaking in the landscape
the castle on the hill
seen dimly through the fog
the mists along the river
flowing silently past
it's current rushing
onward towards the sea
This is life

these still, small moments
that we breathe into
with our silent eyes
Sometimes life is peaceful instead of always pain and we search to recapture that peace again
Each day we are born anew into an awakening world a new chance
to live a new dream
a new opportunity
to join in the dance
Life gives us
many pathways to take wandering here
wandering there
like a stream
flowing down a hill
We can follow
where it leads us
trusting that always
rivers lead to the sea
our silent, sleepless mother beckoning us home
Lit by the moon
the sun or a star
our pathway obscured by dappled shadows
cast by the trees
We go onward slowly lest we not fall
sometimes we stop
in awe of it all
These are the moments that make up a life
moments of stillness
to break up the strife

Feelings of Madness

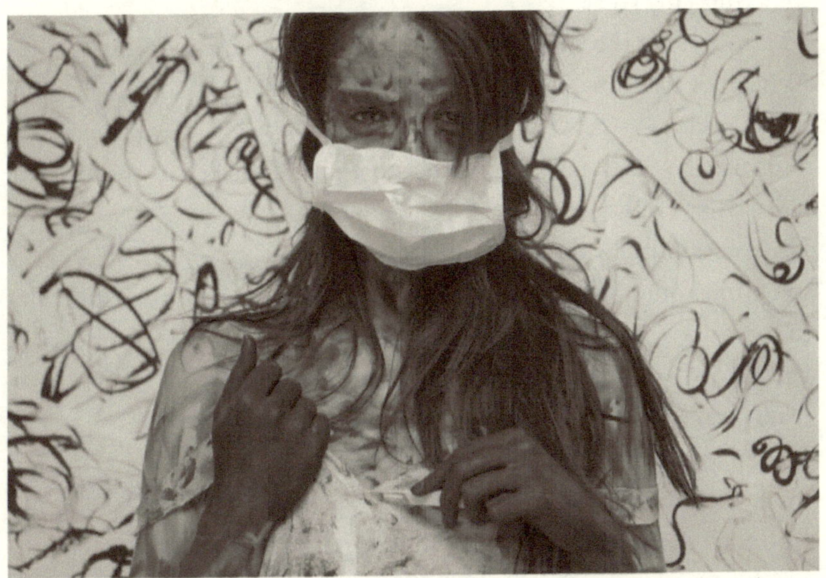

Image byEngin Akyurt[1] from Pixabay[2]

The voices in my head
are like screams
full of sadness
they break the silence
leading to madness
I know why they say
we are all crazy

---

1. **https://pixabay.com/users/engin_akyurt-3656355/?utm_source=link-attribution&utm_medium=referral&utm_campaign=image&utm_content=1838149**
2. **https://pixabay.com/?utm_source=link-attribution&utm_medium=referral&utm_campaign=image&utm_content=1838149**

we try to cope
but the screams
are so loud sometimes
I want to mute
their angry screaming voices
sometimes my voice
                    or the voices of things people said in the past
A litany of madness angry voices
things said
that can't be taken back no matter how much you try to apologize or make things right
The voices still stay for years and years
sometimes quiet whispers but other times so loud they are so difficult to run or avoid
Every horrible thing someone said to me all my life
plays on repeat
again and again
the screams don't stop
And then there is me with my own screams I don't want to be
a bad person
I don't try
to do something wrong it wasn't my intention to hurt you
And my apologies
in moments of clarity don't matter either
it isn't enough
to make up for the past
Screaming, crying
angry sad disgusting mess
It's like my mind is gone it becomes my enemy
even when I shut my eyes
I still hear the screams
There is some escape

when I can finally sleep
find the silence
an end to the pain
Sleep so long
as long as we can
hiding in bed
with the covers up
pulled over my head
Days and days
waiting for the pain to stop
for the screams to die down
to a manageable chatter
Happiness, sadness, love, lust, pain
all of them bleed into just
a little mess in my head
Like a painting
left underwater
until the colors blur
it will never ever
look the same
Ruined mess
that used to be beautiful
looking in the mirror
at my tear stained cheeks
black eye makeup smudge
puffy from crying
it gets hard to breathe
and I feel like
I aimlessly crumble

This is a poem about what it feels like to live with depression. Sometimes your feelings can just become overwhelming, and it seems like the pain is never going to end. It feels like you are drowning and there is no lifeline in sight. I hope this poem can help someone else who has depression to not feel so alone, and anyone who has a loved one who is depressed to understand. Thank you for reading!

Feelings We Don't Want to Confront

Image byИгорь Левченко[1] from Pixabay[2]

Feelings in my heart
that I don't know how
to speak aloud
Like somehow
putting voice to things
gives them power
over my life
I don't want to admit
all the pain I feel

---

1. https://pixabay.com/users/stergo-4163614/?utm_source=link-attribution&utm_medium=referral&utm_campaign=image&utm_content=2049567
2. https://pixabay.com/?utm_source=link-attribution&utm_medium=referral&utm_campaign=image&utm_content=2049567

all the heartbreak
like that will
make it real
I want to hide
alone with the pain
wrapped in a blanket
of sadness and silence
How do I let go
and simultaneously
hold it all in
so no one can see
no one can judge
me as failing
Feeling is failing
in the eyes of the world when your feelings
are dark and brooding instead of happy
like you should be
I have this world
of all the 'shoulds'
placed upon my shoulders for all these years
causing recrimination and so many fears
How do you let go
of the past
so interwoven
with the fabric
of yourself
How do you take apart the things that made you when it is like tearing
apart your own skin
That's what it is like trying to deny
all these feelings
hiding deep within

Finding Our Way Again

Did we ever have it to begin with?

Photo byClay Banks[1] on Unsplash[2]

1. https://unsplash.com/@claybanks?utm_source=medium&utm_medium=referral

2. https://unsplash.com/?utm_source=medium&utm_medium=referral

Our world today is sad we see suffering everywhere when we open our eyes so we close them
to blot out the sun
blot out the suffering
holding back tears
unshed still
after all these years
There is so much to do so much to be
so much to strive for
to make things better
if we only work together if we only try
Can we build
a better future
with these tiny hands?
Can we stop the suffering of these dying lands?
I want to make a difference I want to have a choice I want to make things better I want to have a voice
We cling to what we have in fear of more loss
we stand at a crossroads and still sit here lost

Finding Peace Amidst the Chaos

Photo byDmitry Osipenko[1] on Unsplash[2]

After the chaos of the day
I feel peaceful
calm and centered
ready for the night
and the silence it brings
I feel at rest
still inside
heartbeat quiet
which is rare for me
No anxiety symptoms today all is calm and restful
like the peace after the storm and there are no clouds in the sky today
Everything is shades
of blue that fade to black and the silence of the night comes in with a whisper

1. https://unsplash.com/@dmosipenko?utm_source=medium&utm_medium=referral

2. https://unsplash.com/?utm_source=medium&utm_medium=referral

Forgotten Mysteries

© Kharchenkoirina | Megapixl.com

My vision is clouded
as though there is something
just beyond the edges
that I can almost see
almost coming to light
yet shrouded in darkness
like the memory of a dream
on the edge of awareness
You are almost there
just keep walking
spirit whispers

in the darkness
just a little farther
and you will see
the truth
you have been seeking
Like a memory of the past shadow of another life only half remembered
hanging in the air
fading in the silence
of the early morning
Walking on through the mist to a place unknown
a destination unseen
all is shadows
yet I must press on
ever forward
ever on
A memory of a dream unfinished poems
splash through my memory:
The dreamer lies bleeding inside her bed
in a crystal prison
inside her head
and
broken
I lie sobbing in the rain I drown, I bleed
try to forget the pain
of a thousand yesterdays
Even when I was young I felt so old and tired
like I never really had youth, beauty or freedom only this sense of purpose propelling me forward refusing to stop
no matter how steep
the climb became
The journey of a mystic is never an easy one
don't lie to yourself

and think it is all
sunshine and rainbows
It is crying in the rain
to hide your tears
holding in the pain
you are ashamed to feel
trying to walk alone
faceless through this world but hands clutch at you
with all their neediness
and you can't but help
to answer those cries
the ones that need you
They always need you
always need something
always hands outstretched asking for so much more than you have to give
even as you give your last shred of clothing and
they begin to tear
into your very flesh
Nothing you can do
is ever enough
nothing you can give
will satiate the hunger
Answers must come from inside not from the mystic or
from the teacher
those answers can only
take you halfway there
you must look inside
and find your own soul
find your own peace
your own fulfillment
I cannot ever give you

enough
though I gave you everything I had to give
I am not enough for you
I will never be enough
but you don't know that you don't care
and still you tear
the last of my flesh from unforgiving bone chewing on what is there
until nothing is left

Foundations of Love

Some of us build everything
around those we love
our love is the foundation
for everything in our lives
But other people
look for things
and people
to help them
move forward
somehow unattached
unbound
by chains of love
How do we build our foundation
on sifting sands
washing away
with every crashing tide
with every wave
those sands
carried out to sea
How do we content ourselves
with love that is never enough
to build a firm foundation
laid stone by stone
with two sets of hands
not just one
building alone
Why do I crave love so much

that I never feel fulfilled
how do I ever fill my cup
when it is filled with holes
and the water just runs
out the bottom again
I need a different cup
I need to fill the holes
I need a heart not broken
that feels like it can
hold onto something
instead of always slipping
out through all the cracks
It feels like I was born
with a broken heart
already
when I was young
I still was not enough
I was never whole
I never had legs
strong enough
to stand on
My heart was never whole
always ripped asunder
By not being loved enough
I was just a child then
without a mother's love
without a hand to hold
always alone
in this great, wide world
with no guide
no map to lead me
no compass

to point the way
and no home
to find my way back to
Where am I going
just in circles
leading nowhere
How do you go home
when you never
had one
to start with
How do you find your way
back to yourself
when you never really
existed to start with
I was always
just a shadow
in someone else's dream
never the main character
no matter how it seemed
What do you hold onto
when there is nothing here
just empty days of sadness
alone here with my fear
How do you start again
when all you feel is falling
how do you find a way
when nothing is calling
All there is
is empty silence
alone in these cold walls
here amidst the memories
of other times and other falls

How do you get up again
when you have no legs
to stand on
How do you go forward
when there is no ground
to land on
Always empty
always drowning
Fear, sorrow, regret
have been my constant
and only companions
on this journey
as forward I stumble
through the rains
fighting against demons
trying to ease the pains
So much of the past
was running from demons
running from myself
the darkness within
always a mirror
for the darkness without
How do you ease
the hunger and the pain
of never feeling satisfied
alone here in the rain
Hungry for love
hungry for time
hungry for answers
and wishing
you were mine
You promised answers

long ago that time
you promised solace
and a wish
that you were mine
But you never really
understood my darkness
or felt the very depths
of my endless
aching pain
You couldn't answer
the aloneness
couldn't remember
even my name
I have always been
only hollow inside
unable to hold water
or anything else
that was mine
The only thing I ever
really had was emptiness
and shadows
of a time someday
when that emptiness
would end
Nothing satiates
the hunger or
ends the pain
all of these regrets
don't let me live
yet again
What do I hold onto
when there is nothing

but emptiness here
and there
and everywhere
around me
It is like the map
clears away
around me
leaving only
empty blackness

Fractured Thoughts

Image by Victoria_Watercolor from Pixabay

Fractured thoughts
fractured mind
fractured hope
running out of time
Doesn't matter
what I want
doesn't matter
what I fear
So much of life
in one single tear
dripping down my face
not a smile in sight

only a memory
of misguided light
And I remember happiness as this melancholy sets in leaving only emptiness in its wake
how much more can I give how much can I take
before I give up
and give in to sadness
creeping up on me
Like an old friend
who had become a stranger how do we hold fragile hope and keep out of danger
I long for something more something to give meaning to rambling thoughts
and fragile feelings
I feel all the scars
of the past and the pain sitting outside
and wish it would rain to hide these tears
that come streaming now
How do we make dreams come true when we
have no power over
ourselves or our lives
and outside influence
is always seeping in
to bend us like the wind
Trapped into choices
made in haste
and now in hesitation
long to unmake
How do you change your life when life is so ephemeral and not something you can hold in your hand
it just flows
ever onward like

a rushing stream
carrying you along
in its current
How do you swim to shore against the pull of the water trying to drag you under as you approach the rapids how do you free yourself before being torn asunder

Fragile Dreams

Photo
by Madhu Shesharam on Unsplash

Dreams are fragile things
made of stardust and moonbeams peeking through the cracks of our daily lives
We yearn for something more than the things we can see
we long for love
we long to be free
Sometimes we struggle forward sometimes we limp
but other times we remember that we can run or fly
We are more than this
that we have become
more than the doldrums
of the daily routine
We have stardust in us
we have love by our side
There are dreams inside us that don't want to die
After all these years
we are more than just
the sum of our fears
we can be free
of society's chains
and be something more
Yearning for a new life
we have yet to see
bearing fruit
here in reality
We whisper in the night
a soft spoken prayer
to the moon high above
and the light that it shares
There is stardust and moonbeams in the beat of our hearts
dare we dance here
in the light of the stars

The silence of the night
lets us give voice to our dreams without all the judgement we see from our peers
The world is vast
and we small within it
yet the world has so much to offer to each of us
Love, joy, peace, kindness in the whisper of a lover or the gaze of a friend
the feel of the paper
touched by the pen
Dreams whisper come hither into the dance of the stars leave ordinary behind
and come be something more

Full of Dreams

Photo by Arno Smit on Unsplash

A breath of fresh air comes
into this foggy place
new spring flowers blooming
everywhere on the trees
The world comes alive again
and I come alive with it
waking from hibernation
from these cold months
The breath of spring
on my face feels like
the soft caress
of a lover's hands
Voices of springtime whisper

come play with me
come dance with me
come sing a new song
There is new hope and new life left in my old soul
so much love and promise swirling around in my heart
New life like new love
in the green of the spring and all the baby animals out in the fields of green
Dreaming of summer
and trips to take
dreaming of the ocean
and the splash of the waves
It beckons me
come and play
this ocean as old as time itself yet it makes us feel young it brings a sense of fun
Spring makes me feel young like the whispers of new love gliding like a bird
through the trees
giving me new hope
and a wish for freedom
Locked in the house
all winter
we rest and sleep
but now we awake
coming beautifully alive as the world breathes life into our sleeping forms
I long to move
my legs and run
to dive into the water
and take a swim
walk through paths

filled with wildflowers
Coming alive again
so fresh and new
seeing through new eyes
this same beautiful becoming that happens every year
The world moves in circles in cycles
and so do we
it is time to wake up
time to dream a new dream love a new love
write a new song
dance a new dance
find where we belong

Goddess of Death

The goddess comes to me inside my dreams
sometimes she's crying sometimes she screams
Darkness and pain
anger, hate, fear
all dark emotions
draw Kali near
Living in Kali Yuga the world's dark age how do we live again to turn the page?
History after history reclaim the future
sins of the past
burn in your face
To defeat evil
Shiva created
a darker evil still
Dark goddess mother screams from above finding a new lover
searching for love
How do we find peace to end the dark age
all just the players
on life's big stage
Find a way home
falling from grace
Looking to the stars tracing the age-lace
Follow your dreams follow your star
trust in the future
and be who you are
Transcend the darkness Bring light from the ashes
of hopeless disgrace Climb out of this hole and find a new place
Love, hate, love
longing and loneliness Faith from above

Help the demon remember She was an angel once

Growth is Painful

© Michellemealing | Megapixl.com

My life is like a pair
of worn out shoes
grown too small
and worn with time
but I can't take them off
though they pinch and pain
they are too tight
and too well tied
Like a string around my neck
a hangman's noose
or a bird still sitting
in a too small cage
I have grown
but my life has not
I have changed
in ways they forgot

Time for a change
of scene and something
new
A new path
a new life
to replace the one
That I outgrew
Why does change bring
this sense of loss
so profound
when I hear the call
of the far horizon
I must go forward
without delay
and yet
delay I do
I don't want to go on
without you
Yet here you are
stuck in place
happy without change
I see in your face
Once we were like
those old shoes
we were new
we were beautiful
and a perfect fit
But time has passed
and each shoe
has become somehow
a separate fit
Things once so easy

so playful
and full of fun
have grown worn
and come undone
How do I go forward
on this path alone
without my match
like just one shoe
I need my other half
my other shoe
how can I be
just one alone
out in the world
while you stay home
Yet sometimes
home isn't what
we think it is
and we have to find
the place we fit
Nothing fits here
not for me
I feel trapped
and need to be free
Please come with me
out in the world
walk another path
hold my hand awhile
I can't let go
can't turn my back
walk on without you
I'm just one half
I've tried to cry

I've tried to beg
when reason
and logic failed
I tried to appeal
to your emotional side
Please come with me
I need your strength
I can't go alone
without you beside me
How do I let go
when you are stuck
here in this place
that you want to call home
but leaves me
only broken
like turning leaves
I am falling down
turning from green
to dullish brown
I can't live here
I cannot stay
my home is out there
so far away
You are making a new life
a new pair of shoes
but how can I live
as just one shoe?

Heartbreak

A poem

© **Littlemacproductions**[1] | **Megapixl.com**[2]

My heart breaks a little more
every time I look at you
that once loved face
staring back at me with apathy
as you listen to me cry
Yet again these pointless tears
that drown me in solitude
won't take the pain away
or erase your betrayal
My heart is broken
and I can't fix it when
I am looking into your eyes
fixed silently on me
telling me I should be happy
that everything is fine
But for me
everything is not fine
everything is ruined
and you can't see that
You can't see the depths
of my emptiness and pain
losing you and I am grieving

---

1. **https://www.megapixl.com/littlemacproductions-stock-images-videos-portfolio**

2. **https://www.megapixl.com/**

a love we never shared
But I thought we did
I thought you loved me
all these years
and you let me think it
let me believe we had a future
let me believe your heart
was as true as mine
But it was all just lies
smoke and mirrors
to get me to stay here
Why did you hold me close
all those nights in your arms
when your heart was far away
dreaming of someone else
who could love you better
than I ever could
You let me love you
when you felt nothing
in return for me
You say you didn't lie
but it was a lie of omission
you didn't say you loved me
didn't say that you would stay
But you said we were a family
and had an unshakeable bond
What bond was that
if not love?
Relationships are based on love
and you had none
You just took from me
when you had nothing

to give in return
I gave you everything
all that I have
all that I am
until nothing was left
Now that I am used up
you so easily
discard me
like yesterday's trash
into the rubbish heap
ready to be burned up
Was I really worth
so little to you?
I wasted all these years
all these senseless tears
when your heart
is closed to me forever
How can you ask me
to stay here
when you break my heart
again each time
I look at your face
Don't you see
that you broke my heart
broke my mind
broke my soul
And now I am too old
to make another life
without you
You took away
all the time
when I was young

and could have found
a heart as true
as mine
who would have held me
and sheltered me
when I grew old
You took that from me
the opportunity
to find real love
because I sat here
with you
and you didn't love me

How do you Erase the Pain?

A poem

Photo byFa Barboza[1] on Unsplash[2]

How do you erase the pain
etched in every cell of your body
by the tears of the past
and the fears of the future
We walk always
into the unknown
searching through the blackness
for a hand to hold our own
Sometimes we stop to wonder
how we can appreciate life more
and there are beautiful moments
that make it all feel worthwhile
But why are those moments
so few and far between
and why do we spend so much time
wasted being less than
our very best selves
to the ones we love
How do you know
you love someone enough
for them to love you back
with the same ferocity

1. https://unsplash.com/@fan11?utm_source=medium&utm_medium=referral

2. https://unsplash.com/?utm_source=medium&utm_medium=referral

When do you decide
that what you are getting
just isn't enough
for it to be sustainable
How do you know
that this person
is your forever person
when they don't know
that you are the one
for them
Is good enough
actually anything
to anyone
ever
Or is it just a cop out
because we don't want
to really be alone
How do you know
if the hand you hold
through the darkness
of the night
doesn't belong
to a ghost
a fragment of something
that is already gone
Do you believe in soulmates
or that we have this one love
that is meant to complete us
Or do some of us
just end up alone
no matter what we do
or how hard we love

I want to be enough
to have the strength
to hold onto your hand
and walk onward
from the darkness
into the light
I have to trust
that the light is there
at the end of the tunnel
somewhere
How do we know
that the light is real
and that it isn't just
a lie we tell ourselves
to keep moving forward

How Do You Heal A Broken Heart?

Image bySeaReeds[1] from Pixabay[2]
How do you heal a broken heart
when it is still in the process
of breaking
torn open again every day
by racing thoughts
and feelings of confusion
knowing what you want
and that you can't have it
when other people's feelings
are so much involved
You can't unmake choices
either yours or theirs
and hearts are connected
but still frozen
locked in place with
decisions made
so rigidly
I wish I could change
your heart or your mind
I wish I could turn back time

---

1. https://pixabay.com/users/searceds-536040/?utm_source=link-attribution&utm_medium=referral&utm_campaign=image&utm_content=571968
2. https://pixabay.com/?utm_source=link-attribution&utm_medium=referral&utm_campaign=image&utm_content=571968

and do something differently
so we could all be together
now torn apart
seemingly forever
and it stings inside
I wish for a comprimise
from either side
that isn't coming
and I am stuck
here in the middle
longing to bring us together
once again
How do you seek forgiveness
for things gone so wrong
in so many ways
on so many sides
and the forgiveness needed
isn't only yours
How do you make a consensus
when no one else wants one
and they each stand
by choices they have made
it is only me here with regret
for the way things have been
It feels lonely here
stuck in the middle of things
that I cannot hope to change
I feel a sense of lostness
and resignation
wishing still
that the answer would change
but they still just say no

and I still just feel stuck
Throwing a breath of hope
into the wind now
asking something greater
to help me find change
and a softening of hearts
a magical way to fix things
that I have no answers for
I need to trust in something more
to bring about the changes
that I seek so deeply
Something bigger than myself
the Universe or God
I beg to save me now
from this nightmare
of my own making
and so many things
that I can't undo
I whisper a silent prayer
to somehow make this right
to make the past come undone
and let us walk into the light

I Already Told You

Image byPetra[1] from Pixabay[2]
Yeah, at the end I ghosted
but the thing is
there was nothing left
I didn't already say
a hundred times before
and I realized
even when I did speak
you never listened
anyway
Everything was always
all about you
about your feelings
your wants and needs
and the ways I fell short
You told me you didn't want me
so what was I supposed to say
after that
I guess it's all just
aftermath anyway
What's the point

1. https://pixabay.com/users/pezibear-526143/?utm_source=link-attribution&utm_medium=referral&utm_campaign=image&utm_content=1390586
2. https://pixabay.com/?utm_source=link-attribution&utm_medium=referral&utm_campaign=image&utm_content=1390586

of saying goodbye?
of telling you one last time
how much you hurt me
and listing all the times
that you fell short
of acting something
like a human
much less my mother
You never loved me
not like you loved *her*
my sister
That time I saw you
hold her while she cried
I thought to myself damn
why could that never
ever be me?
You were never the one
to heal my tears
cried alone in the dark
muffled into my pillow
so no one would hear them
No, more often
you were the cause of them
So young
the first time
you told me to be quiet
to go away
And I didn't even
go play
No, I went and cried
in the dark hallway
covering my mouth

so no sound
would come out
I got good at that
got good at being silent
at hiding my pain
painting on a smile
pretending to be fine
You already know
all the ways you hurt me
Once I was old enough
I told you every time
I called you out
said no bitch
it isn't fine anymore
I'm not a child
I'm not a puppet
I don't have to take
your abuse anymore
I am a person
deserving of respect
just like every other
person on the planet
I told you I wanted
to fix our relationship
to talk about feelings
like normal
mom and daughter
But you told me
"our family doesn't do that"
and when I pressed you said
"I hate your ex-husband"
thanks mom

for again
making it all
about you
Like when you told me
you were traumatized
that time at the beach
when your negligent ass
let my daughter get hurt
Life with you
was always only
ever about you
I was just like
a paper doll
for you to play with
one dimensional
without feelings
without purpose
without a backstory
I didn't get
to be a person
So many things
you did that hurt me
said that hurt me
times you ignored me
times I begged for help
and you told me
my problems were
my fault
You are narcissistic trash
and when you take out the trash
you just throw it out
without a backward glance

I Love Fiercely

©Grandfailure[1] |Megapixl.com[2]

When I love
I love fiercely
protecting those I love
at any cost
Take my hand
and walk with me
through the fire
I will hold you close
your hand in mine
I will protect you
until my last breath
I will keep you safe
against any storm
When I love
my love is like fire
it is all-consuming
I love with every fiber of my being
from the depths of my heart
with the entirety of my immortal soul
I don't know how
to love halfway
to be unsure
to hold back

1. https://www.megapixl.com/grandfailure-stock-images-videos-portfolio

2. https://www.megapixl.com/

a piece of myself
When I love you
I love you with everything
I don't know how to love
any other way
Sometimes it hurts
to love so fiercely
in a world
where others don't
To be always
the one who loves more
tears away pieces
of my heart and soul
leaving scars
where past loves
used to be held
When you love with everything
losing that love means
losing everything
It means having your soul
rent in two
when love fails you
and love often does
Yet still I love
and I love fully
either all the way
or not at all
Children, lovers, friends, family
I hold them all cradled
here inside my soul
Even when I regret you
still, I can't forget you

Sometimes in the night
memories come in dreams
dark as if lit
only by firelight
seen from far away
somewhere in the distance
whispers of your name
a shadow of your face
and it reminds me
of the piece of my heart
you stole long ago
Maybe you left it
somewhere along the way
that scrap of my heart
torn like the fabric
of a tattered old scarf
set free in the wind
winding its way
through desert sands
never to return to me
or my fragile hands

I Love You More

Photo byaranprime[1] on Unsplash[2]
When I fell in love
with you
I loved you more
than anyone else
I had ever loved
before
I fell in love
with your kindness
your beautiful soul
your eyes
your smile
the curve of your hips
the way you held me tight
in the middle
of the long night
I loved you with everything
I had to give inside
my heart
my soul
I was honest with you
about everything
my heart
my feelings

1. https://unsplash.com/@aranprime?utm_source=medium&utm_medium=referral

2. https://unsplash.com/?utm_source=medium&utm_medium=referral

my pain
my hurt
my shame
I laid myself bare
before you
speaking words
of truth
in a way I never had
to anyone else
When we fought
I stayed
I tried to work things out
I didn't run
like I always did before
It was hard to stay
hard to be honest
hard to be open
to try to forgive
the hurts of the past
when I had been hurt
so much by life already
What we have
was supposed to be
just a summer fling
before you moved away
but you stayed
all this time
you stayed
No one had ever
stayed with me
before
So many firsts with you

though I had loved others
before we met
I never loved anyone
the way that I loved you
And I still do
I still love you
with everything inside
though time and distance
separate us now
my love
you are my heart
you are my always
and forever love
The love I loved the most
the love that makes me more
inspires me to be better
and to become more whole
Alone into the night
I whisper your name
waiting for the time
we can be together again

I Used to be a Different Person

Image owned by Author
Letter from an old friend
sparks memories this morning
waking from sleep and
troubled dreams
Sometimes the past
feels so long ago
and we don't look back
as often as we once did
That is progress but
do we forget how far
we have actually gone?
Do we forget the faces
the places of the past
as we look ever forward
towards the mountain top
where our dreams lie waiting?
Is it a bad thing to change?
In my case,
I think not.
There are things I was
when I was haunted
by all those shadows
that I didn't want to be
Instead of being
fragile and broken
I used anger to be strong

I kept going for years
without taking a breath
without taking a pause
to just be with myself
Now I have that pause
now I have that silence
a chance to mend
the broken heart and mind
time to find my soul again
time to renew the strength
that had waned to nothing
I have a chance now to be
the caterpillar entering
the cocoon
to become the butterfly
when I wake
from this dream
Now I have a chance
to become who I always
dreamed I could be
Now I have choices
about what I do
who I see
where I go
no one forces me
like they did for
so many years before
I have a chance to look
in the mirror and see
my real face again
instead of just a mask
of makeup

I see me in realness
I see my pain and scars
but I see beauty too
and the same eyes
looking back at me
across all these years
Things change
we change
and life moves
in circles and cycles
taking us back to
the same lessons again
now that we are wiser
and ready to understand
the things we always knew

I Will Never Be

©Olgabrik[1] |Megapixl.com[2]

I will never be
normal like you
want me to be
My face is not
the perfect face
that you crave
My hands
little and scarred
don't reach
far enough
My feet don't
walk fast enough
to keep up
with your quick steps
always going faster
trying to catch up
That's my whole life
playing catch up
Trying to be enough
trying to be better
to make you happy
to make you love me
I wanted to be worthy

---

1. https://www.megapixl.com/olgabrik-stock-images-videos-portfolio
2. https://www.megapixl.com/

just as I am
to be loved and accepted
not to feel dirty
But I just feel
too small
Always trying
to somehow
catch up
Not good enough
strong enough
brave enough
pretty enough
fun enough
smart enough
I just want
what I am
to be enough
for someone
I just wanted
to be loved
for being me
instead of always trying
to be something more
something beautiful
something whole
Why am I not
a whole person
just this tiny
broken doll
missing something
But what is missing?
what is always

so wrong
about me?
I don't know
how to fix it
how to be better
how to deserve
to be treated
like more

I'm Not a Fiction Writer

I have seen too much of reality to create another world

Photo bySixteen Miles Out[1] on Unsplash[2]

What I write
it's not enough
to convey my heart
the sentiments I feel
I have seen too much
felt too much
become immersed
in this world of ours
the gray and the green
the love and the hate
the fearfulness and longing
that makes us who we are
instead of who we
wish to be
We aspire to be more
to do more
to be better
than we think we are
we make our angelic souls
so fragile
marked with tears
into something hateful

1. https://unsplash.com/@sixteenmilesout?utm_source=medium&utm_medium=referral

2. https://unsplash.com/?utm_source=medium&utm_medium=referral

as we fight through the years
Time passes
seasons change
but this longing in our souls
that stays the same
The longing for something else
something true, something more
something to silence
the screams in the night
a balm
to ease the endless pain
Life is beautiful
but so much of life is pain
so much of ourselves
is tied up to loneliness
to chances lost
and words unsaid
We want to be something else
something beautiful
that we were born to be
but from an early age
we learn the world
is a place that leaves scars
a place that causes tears
and the people we love
let us down the most
because we expect
too much of them
We long to be cared for
tenderly, like a child
but even children now
aren't cradled in our arms

they are torn away
going to daycare
while we chase the dollar
Another day, another woe, another tower went up, where the homeless had their home. ~ Jewel
We try to save ourselves
and each other
from drowning
in this endless black sea
But there is no shore
in sight of this boat
no matter how far
we row or we go
is it waterworld?
have we destroyed the earth
with climate change?
Are we living in
humanity's aftermath?
the decline of civilization
as it once was known?
is that why nowhere
can feel like home?
All the buildings blown away
all the windows bombed out
we live in the fallout
of an age of apathy
too late for wisdom
too broken for anger
we just row on
in this little boat
seeking
seeking something more

Inner Darkness

I have so much inner darkness
it spills out at the seams
cracks in the façade
the face that I share
the mask I hide behind
is what I always wear
Awake from this dream of evil
and fly
somewhere far away from here
the place of your loss
the home of your sadness
the scars on your heart
Can you unbreak
what has been shattered?
can you find yourself
among the shards
of what is left
of the life you built
so long ago
Broken angel
broken wings
put it back together
with broken fingers
Like a glass figurine
you have shattered
and been stepped on
by passerby in the street

Your name forgotten
your pain spilled out
your misspent years
gliding by in silence
no one sees your tears
no one sees your real face
You have nothing left
everything spilled out
blood spattered walls
where the paint has cracked
left you forgotten
long, long ago
But you remember
you are still here
silent as a ghost
looking through the mirror
The pain that once was
like a whisper of time
fades on the wind
as you silently fade

Learning Acceptance

Photo byDeniz Altindas[1] on Unsplash[2]

Learning to accept
your lot in life
can be difficult
when you don't want
to be where you are
and you feel like
you miss your home
more than anything
in the world
What can you do
when your heart is broken
and needs to be fixed
somehow, some way
We need to go home
to where we came from
back to the stardust
that is the breath
of the universe
Surrender to the silence
inside your soul
accept your unhappiness
accept your lot in life
Life isn't fair

1. https://unsplash.com/@omeganova?utm_source=medium&utm_medium=referral

2. https://unsplash.com/?utm_source=medium&utm_medium=referral

and when we expect it to be
we set ourselves up for disappointment
It is ok to be disappointed
it is ok to be sad
and to feel your heart break
The loss of something
empties out your soul
to find higher realization
You have to be empty
before you can get full
so what do you use
to fill in the holes
in your broken life?
Is it more love?
more compassion?
more stillness?
How do we find acceptance
of our own suffering
as the natural state of things?
Watch your dreams die
watch yourself die
from the outside
the death of the ego
so the soul can live
We transform like butterflies
wrapped in a cocoon
the death of one life
so we can learn to fly
Letting go completely
of our hopes and expectations
so that we can find something
completely new

to heal us

Life in Freefall

Photo byBruce Christianson[1] on Unsplash[2]

I am in freefall
tumbling precariously
through thin air
with nothing beneath
except more air
Where am I going
spinning out of control
what lies at the bottom
when I finally hit
will my touchdown be soft
or will it bring death
Out of control
nothing to grab onto
no hand to hold
no one to save me
and only darkness below
Everything is blackness
and I feel sheer terror
mixed with resignation
a scream passes my lips
and fades away to silence
I can't hold on to anything
there is nothing here

1. https://unsplash.com/@photologic?utm_source=medium&utm_medium=referral

2. https://unsplash.com/?utm_source=medium&utm_medium=referral

all alone
in this dark void
the space of the night
the black of the trees
where will I land
falling forever
Crash, bang
I feel myself hit a tree
branch after branch
cutting at me
Finally I hit the ground
with a hard thud
a carpet of grass below
has broken my freefall

Life Leaves Scars

Photo byHannah Xu[1] on Unsplash[2]
Sometimes life leaves scars
on our hearts
on our minds
on our bodies
Things happen
and we are forever changed
by a thought or an action
a word or a fragment
of something that happened
There are things in life
that we can't take back
no matter how much
we regret them
I feel wounded now
by the past
and by the pain
of choices made
in haste and
wishful thinking
We always hope
for the best but
life seldom turns out
the way we have planned

1. https://unsplash.com/pt-br/@ohshoothannah?utm_source=medium&utm_medium=referral

2. https://unsplash.com/?utm_source=medium&utm_medium=referral

or the way we dreamed
Letting dreams die
bleeding in your hands
when you feel your heart
breaking with every beat
is watching your very soul
wither away and die
You know your life
will never be what
you dreamed of
for yourself
or the people around you
and you feel the weight
of others expectations
like a chain
around your neck
like a rock
dragging you down
to the bottom of the ocean
As you drown
in the black uncaring sea
under a moonless sky
you reach up a hand
but no one is there
to catch you
at the depths
to which you have fallen
You are surrounded
in only blackness
no matter where you turn
there is just black water
and your lungs begin to fill

the pain burns inside you
drowning in sorrows
and past regrets
What can the future hold
when there is nothing left
to bring you to the shore
so far out of sight
Only more pain
more sadness and suffering
waits in your life ahead
because the only things
that mattered have gone
so far out of reach
and you are drowning

Longing is Older than Love

Photo byGreg Rakozy[1] on Unsplash[2]

We look out at the stars
and we dream of
something more
somewhere out there
where we can go
and things
will be different
than this mundane world
So much life spent
waiting for the perfect
time, place, person
how do we know
when it arrives?
How do we know when
today will be our day
when it is the day
that suddenly
our dreams arrive
by chance or coincidence
long awaited
silent whispers
into the night
Things we are afraid

1. https://unsplash.com/@grakozy?utm_source=medium&utm_medium=referral

2. https://unsplash.com/?utm_source=medium&utm_medium=referral

in our hearts to speak
and things we don't know
how to make real
How do we know
life's meaning and purpose
when we go in these
seemingly endless loops
that take us right back
to where we started
Older and wiser maybe
are we enlightened
or just tired
some days it is both
some days neither
But other days bring
new hope and excitement
in more whispers
out of the dark
and we wonder
where they come from
answers to prayer?
And we circle forward
again this time faster
going back and back
again and again
to the same places
same faces and it feels
like the excitement
has worn off suddenly
Something new becomes old
something cherished habit
and we long for that next

glimpse over the next hill
to somewhere new
somewhere never seen
that is always where
dreams and mystery wait
in the unseen
the unheard
the uncharted
Craving new beginnings
fresh starts
new goals
new friends
new lovers
new routines
new revelations
Or is it just always
more of the same?

Love Carves a Hole into Your Being

©Inarik[1] |Megapixl.com[2]

Love carves a hole inside us
that is difficult to fill
with anything but love itself
so what do we do then
when love seems to fade
or loved ones are far away
How do we fill that hole
inside ourselves
like a gaping bleeding wound
right there inside my chest
I want to know how
to make it stop hurting
how to make love flow again
or how to bring back
the raging fire of passion
that used to be inside
Lovers, friends, children
all of them in some way
fill this hole with love
and yet our longing
can reach inside too
and fill us with something else
Longing is the pain

---

1. https://www.megapixl.com/inarik-stock-images-videos-portfolio

2. https://www.megapixl.com/

of love unrequited
it is the silence
where music used to play
it is the stillness
where there used to be a dance
and with this longing
comes a frail sadness
We know that love
is possible
because we had it once
we had it but now
it all feels far away
My gaping empty heart
longs to be full again
so how do I fill it?
Can I learn to love
myself enough
to heal the wounds
left by other hands?
Can I love myself enough
to fill this empty hole
here inside my chest
caved in by love lost
and all that is gone
all that is past
Lovers and friends
children and family
gone away and faded
into the background
of my life for now
But just for now
I know I will see them again

I just don't know the when
and that brings the longing
that brings this pain unrequited
I long for your much loved faces
seen in the places of our youth
and I long to see you again
and to hear you speak the truth
that love is everlasting
like the moon, sun or tides
and even though it ebbs and flows
it always comes back
here to fill this hole
inside my heart
I will see you again my lovelies
I will hold you against my chest
I will walk with you again
for a while down the path
before we diverge again
to go our own ways
Because love is the answer
to all the questions that we ask
and it always comes back to us
in some form or fashion
even if not in the ways
that we at first expected
I long for you across this great
expanse of the sea
I long to see your face
to hear your voice
my child, my heart
I long for you always
though you are far away

And the friends who
are like sisters to me
I long for them too
long to have that time together
where we can talk about anything
do anything or nothing
and have the greatest time
I long for you my loves
though you are far away
my heart is full of you
full of this longing
mingled with lasting love
and I want you back
I want you forever
so that we can be together
once again on that distant shore
the ocean calls me home
it calls me to your hearts
whispering my name
in the silence of the night
I long for my homeland
stranger in this strange place
I long for my loves there
and I need to return to grace

Love Me With Softness

Image byVictoria[1] from Pixabay[2]
Love me with softness
shelter me
in the strength
of your arms
Hold me close
but not too tightly
lest I suffocate
I have been loved
roughly before
cast aside
like an worn out
piece of clothing
used up
and with nothing left
inside except scars
I need to be loved
softly now
as I grow older
I am less resilient
now than when

---

1. https://pixabay.com/users/vika_glitter-6314823/?utm_source=link-attribution&utm_medium=referral&utm_campaign=image&utm_content=5120139
2. https://pixabay.com/?utm_source=link-attribution&utm_medium=referral&utm_campaign=image&utm_content=5120139

I wore a younger face
I have grown old
grown tired
of this place
In my weariness
I need love
that is soft
like a blanket
Hands that caress
softly like the wind
Whispers softly
in my ear
speaking tenderness
Love me softly now
love me with gentleness
smooth off all
my rough edges
until I am soft too

My Quiet Morning

Photo byFahmi Fakhrudin[1] on Unsplash[2]
The silence of the early morning
seems to speak to me in whispers
voices telling me that today
is going to be a better day
hang in there baby
it's going to be fine
Look at how far you have come
from where you used to be
it is all about the journey
and the memories that you make
along the way
Life is funny sometimes
the things we think about
or deem as important
the things we do
that are so counterproductive
yet we do move forward
in the in-betweens
Sometimes I look at life
look at myself and
I am surprised at the changes
surprised by how far I have come
all this way from a home

---

1. https://unsplash.com/@fahmipaping?utm_source=medium&utm_medium=referral

2. https://unsplash.com/?utm_source=medium&utm_medium=referral

that I used to know
once upon a time
And the silence of this morning
brings a sense of clarity
a sense of peace
a sense of expectation
Knowing the next chapter
yet unwritten
will be beautiful
and bring me forward
to the light of a new day
Every day shines
if you allow it to be so
and if you get out
of your own way
with overthinking
You have all the answers
inside you already
and you have the wisdom
you have the love
to make this life shine bright
it is your birthright
this sense of joy and peace
the flowing of the breeze
an gentle knowing
that things will work out
and it will all be alright

My Stupid Heart

Photo byMartin Vysoudil[1] on Unsplash[2]
I let my stupid heart
get broken again
by caring about people
who don't care about
other people
I think about things
like world peace and
ending world poverty
and all you care about
is buying more
for yourself
How did I get so deluded
into thinking you were kind
when all along
you never cared
about me
or about anything real
There is real suffering
out there in the world
but why does it seem
like I am the only one
who sees it
who is heartbroken

---

1. https://unsplash.com/@vysix?utm_source=medium&utm_medium=referral

2. https://unsplash.com/?utm_source=medium&utm_medium=referral

by the pain of others
Yes my own pain
has caved into my being
and created compassion
instead of hardening
against the things I see
I choose compassion and love
that was never given to me
because I know no other
should suffer this much
No one should be expected
to walk brokenly on
without another shoulder
to lean on
I choose compassion
out of the fear that I feel
I choose to be honest
and to show what's real
How do so many people
get so wrapped up
in all the minutia
and think that it matters
What you care about
speaks volumes
about your character
don't you want to have
a good one
Don't you want to be remembered
as someone who loved
to the capacity of what love
can truly be in this world
Don't you want to be seen

by your children
as an example
for them to emulate
Don't you want to make the world
as bright and beautiful
as it can be
Why do so many people
care so little
but I still
care so much
about them

My Suicide Note to the Fucking World

© Petro[1] | Megapixl.com[2]

I can't do this anymore.
This.
Life.
Anything.
It is all too hard.
Too painful.
My heart is broken
Too many times
I am so tired
From too many lies
Too much screaming
Too much pain
Too much crying
The endless emptiness
Has seared its way
Into my soul
I have taken care of you
As best as I could
But I realize now
It was never enough
You needed more
Always more
And I can't give you
Any more

1. https://www.megapixl.com/petro-stock-images-videos-portfolio
2. https://www.megapixl.com/

I have nothing left
No help
No hope
Only silence
And a hope
That the pain will fade
You have left me scars
My body battered
Covered in scars
Left broken
Left for dead
But I wasn't dead
So I lie here
Waiting for the end

Not Good Enough

Image byStefan Keller[1] from Pixabay[2]
I get so tired
of being not good enough
of starving for love
and having my heart
crushed
The things you say
run through my head
on repeat
Theatrical
Manipulative
Attention-Seeking
But it isn't
this is me
the true me
and I don't know
how you didn't
always see
My black heart
charred and burned
inside my chest

1. https://pixabay.com/users/kellepics-4893063/?utm_source=link-attribution&utm_medium=referral&utm_campaign=image&utm_content=5501796
2. https://pixabay.com/?utm_source=link-attribution&utm_medium=referral&utm_campaign=image&utm_content=5501796

like a remnant
of a forgotten possibility
a path not taken
a life not lived
Defined by choices
not my own
never my own woman
never my own person
never autonomous
Maybe I never
really had a soul
Or maybe it died
the moment I was born
not good enough
never good enough
never loved
never cared for
my feelings
never spared
It was always your goals
that made things work
made things go forward
You pushed my feet
moved my lips to speak
in all these endless patterns
that went nowhere
I tried to take your path
but there is no coming back
nothing left alive
inside my soul
just blackness
anger, regret and greed

a desire for vengeance
is not what I need
Yes hurt people
hurt people
I get it now
We leave scars
on other hearts
of people
who still have them
Everything is suffering
everything is pain
played out on the stage
always ends the same
Why am I so hopeless
Why am I so dead
still I cannot live
cannot die
in a purgatory
of my own mind
broken
fragmented
lost
insane

Open Your Heart

Photo byJay Castor[1] on Unsplash[2]
Open your heart
feel it unfolding
like a beautiful,
thousand-petaled lotus
feel the softness
of your beauty exposed
Your heart is a wonder
it is the key
to the truest part
of your very soul
the door
to your innermost being
Image byKhusen Rustamov[3] from Pixabay[4]
The door you seek to open
to the truth
is deep inside you
and on the inner journey
you find yourself

---

1. https://unsplash.com/@jayicastor?utm_source=medium&utm_medium=referral
2. https://unsplash.com/?utm_source=medium&utm_medium=referral
3. https://pixabay.com/users/xusenru-1829710/?utm_source=link-attribution&utm_medium=referral&utm_campaign=image&utm_content=1725041
4. https://pixabay.com/?utm_source=link-attribution&utm_medium=referral&utm_campaign=image&utm_content=1725041

already on the path
Your soul is waiting for you
to forget who you
used to be
to drop the mask
let go the facade
and become
who you always were
You are the light
you are the love
you are the spirit
the Self
at the center
of your being
Stop seeking outside
for answers
you already hold
it is just distraction
and only leads
to further confusion
Remember
the things that
you already know
to be deeply true
Remember
the core of yourself
the light that you are
the beauty of you
Stop hiding the light
under a barrel
let it shine brightly
into the vast darkness

Help this world to see
the truth of it all
hiding inside
each of our souls
Come awake
come alive
walk the path
of the soul
Remember
remember
remember
You already know
the deepest truth
You already know
inside yourself
is the vastness
of all that is
You are connected
to the wisdom
of the Self
of the Soul
Awake from the dream
no longer do you need
to silently scream
Heal the pain
open your eyes
all you have to do
is look in the mirror
and see your own face

Passion in Your Soul

Photo bySaiph Muhammad[1] on Unsplash[2]
Do you ever feel your soul
coming alive with passion
a new start of something
that could be wonderful
new possibilities
opening up before you
that you never imagined
Starting a new book
for me is like taking
a new lover
I am completely immersed
in excitement for
my new shiny object
filled with hope
at the magic to come
to the pages unfolding
It is magic being made
taking shape in my hands
words being breathed
into life on the page
falling from my fingertips
like dewdrops
A new world being created

1. https://unsplash.com/@saiph?utm_source=medium&utm_medium=referral

2. https://unsplash.com/?utm_source=medium&utm_medium=referral

a new life taking form
like the birth of a child
it is gestating in my womb
unborn as yet and nurtured
by my own heartbeat
my own breath giving life
A sense of anticipation
as the pages take form
trying to get everything right
make everything just so
a story to hold someone's gaze
Look at me lovely
see this dream I am building
let it take you away
into the starlight
let it be a dream for you too
let it create a new world
where you can fly
on the wings of angels
That is what you are
a beautiful bright angel
and I want my words
to remind you to fly

Reflections in the Glass

Image byN-Y-C[1] from Pixabay[2]
She looks in the mirror
staring into her own eyes
seeing deeply
into her soul
pondering the mysteries
of it all
We dance through the dream
we look for answers
though not what they seem
seeing in those eyes
are all the answers
to the history of humanity
And just one question
at the beginning of it all
Why, she asks herself
why am I here all alone?
What is the meaning of this
of life, of love, of anything
why do I yearn for something more
why do I feel like life

1. https://pixabay.com/users/n-y-c-8156946/?utm_source=link-attribution&utm_medium=referral&utm_campaign=image&utm_content=3179182
2. https://pixabay.com/?utm_source=link-attribution&utm_medium=referral&utm_campaign=image&utm_content=3179182

is beyond the next shore
why do I never find
anything to end this yearning
Longing is older than love
they say
gazing at the mirror
of magic far away
You see a figure
far ahead on the trail
chasing after her
like a cat
chasing its own tail
Are you following
your own shadow
around in a circle?
Are the footsteps
you follow your own
left long ago
when you began your search
and you passed this way
once before
Two sets of footprints
traced in the sand now
and both of them
are really yours
You look for a god
or a goddess in the dream
not knowing your reflection
is more than what it seems
The answers are your own
etched upon your heart
left there at the beginning

when you were there before
Creation and destruction
walking hand in hand
the angel and the demon
walk this foreign land
Seeking for our home
in the place that we forgot
a journey ever onward
circling the earth
again and again
wearing a new face
yet we circle back again
not recognizing that this
is still the same place
Nothing new under the sun
no matter how long we bake
no answers in the moonlight
though we wait for it to rise
we seek an end to separation
for some kind of reprise
A new song to sing
a new love to make us feel
our quest to unbreak time
to end the endless wheel
Where do we go from here
as we wander place to place
looking for an answer
behind another strange face
An echo of our goddess self
left from long ago
a memory of a golden age
when we knew where to go

Walking as if asleep
half in a trance
we look in the mirror
and our hair is askance
These strange eyes
gazing back from the mirror
blue to green to black
they fade through the haze of time
still silently looking back
This life or the next life
as we move from dream to dream
learning another lesson
trying to drown our own screams
muffled in my throat
they rise in fear now
and desperation
crying out for more
in our abandonment
we look for something else
we seek for something true
But how do we know
the truth when full circle
we have gone yet again
and gone no where new
We have seen everything
that the sun can light in our path
we have trodden every road
and still we circle back

Remember to Forget

Photo byRyan Parker[1] on Unsplash[2]
Remember to forget
forget to remember
always we circle on
circle forward
circle back
till we find
our way home
to the place
which is not
To the shores
of that great sea
with the white ships
departing across
that endless ocean
We look to the sea
the crashing of the waves
against the great cliffs
and we wonder
what comes after
what came before
and we have memory
glimpses of other lives
glimpses of other worlds

---

1. https://unsplash.com/@dryanparker?utm_source=medium&utm_medium=referral
2. https://unsplash.com/?utm_source=medium&utm_medium=referral

that lie far away
across that great sea
Is it a metaphor somehow
for the vastness of the galaxy
and all those glowing stars
the place of our birth
far away but not yet
forgotten
How do we get back home
to the place that we came from
do we want to go there
or do we go forward now
in the place where we are
Is it a blessing or a curse
to remember the other world
the world that came before
and all the strange things
that we cannot seem to understand
All the other lives
all the other memories
where do they lead us?

Remembering Who I Used to Be

©Darrenbaker[1] |Megapixl.com[2]

Trying to remember who I was
before I felt so sad
before this blackness came
smothering me like
a pillow in the night
leaving me unable to breathe
much less function
in any normal way
My heart feels broken
my soul feels lost
my body is adrift
on this endless sea
Floating on waves of time
on this tiny wooden plank
waiting for someone
to come and rescue me
left without a paddle
far from any shore
so distant now
as to be unseen
Sitting in the emptiness
of space and time
watching them pass by

---

1. https://www.megapixl.com/darrenbaker-stock-images-videos-portfolio
2. https://www.megapixl.com/

but not participating
My thoughts tumble
on endless repeat in my mind
regret and recriminations
and all the things you said
How do I get back to somewhere
where there is earth
beneath my feet again
even if it isn't home
a shore where I can stop
this endless waking dream
where nothing seems real
and I wish I was asleep
I want to come back to myself
to the person I used to be
when I used to be happy
or at least a bit peaceful
and I had some insights
into this life of mine
Everything feels faded
and far away
like photos taken
in black and white
their edges yellowing
in the heat of the sun
the pictures fading with
years that pass
faces unrecognizable
only outlines now
I feel like a cardborad cut-out
of a person I used to be
like I am only

two dimensional now
flat on both sides
only pretending to stand
and unable to move
No touch of a hand
no breath of the air
nothing to stir the stillness
that I feel everywhere

Searching for Peace

Photo bySunguk Kim[1] on Unsplash[2]

I am searching
for a sense of peace
that seems elusive
here
in this strange place
A world far from home
so much is lost
so much is gone
and some days
the change
is just too much
it's exhausting
and suffocating
and just peeking
my head out of bed
feels too much
How do I find
my way back
to my spirit
to myself
the path seems lost
with twists and turns
and unfamiliar signs

1. https://unsplash.com/@sunyu?utm_source=medium&utm_medium=referral

2. https://unsplash.com/?utm_source=medium&utm_medium=referral

things I can't read
that probably
tell where to go
But where
am I supposed
to go anyway?
Isn't peace
supposed to be
inside us all?
Quiet the mind
the monks say
release your thoughts
sit by the bank
of the rushing stream
find yourself
separate
from your thoughts
they are not you
But what about when
you have anxiety
and depression
and those thoughts
are like screams
following you everywhere
The monks didn't write
about intrusive thoughts
that you can't shake
Like a sea monster
in that little stream
the waters dark
you stifle a scream
as it pulls you down

you know not where
and water
fills your lungs
drowning
drowning
drowning
That is my only thought
I am drowning
I cannot breathe
my lungs are burning
So much pain
and then it all
just fades
to blackness
Did the monks
write about that?
All they said
is life is suffering
even a child
knows the truth
of that
Yes there is a path
leading from suffering
but even on the path
I suffer still
clawing my way
blindly onward
lying on my belly
slowly I crawl
I know inner peace
is our true nature
so how do I get free

from the outer turmoil
to go within
when everything in my life
needs so much attention
and the screams
are with real
voices now
voices always asking
for something more
their needs
never satiated
How do I break free
of the needs
of this world
to meet my own
small need
to be free

Seeking Silence

Photo bySandro Gonzalez[1] on Unsplash[2]
Seeking the silence of the soul
and the space where we find ourselves
all one self
Love and oneness
that is what we are
this vast heart
in the fabric
of the universe
How do we describe
the cessation of self
as we dissolve
into the boundless self
Over and over
like ice cubes that
freeze and melt
We freeze and melt back
many times into the ocean
water remembers its shape
as it changes form
Yet we forget ours
as we go from place to place
instead of searching within
to find the silence of ourselves

---

1. https://unsplash.com/@sandro?utm_source=medium&utm_medium=referral

2. https://unsplash.com/?utm_source=medium&utm_medium=referral

Let go of yourself
your wants
your needs
your dreams
your fears
Let go of everything
and what is left
that is YOU

Self Doubt

Photo byM.[1] on Unsplash[2]
A sense of self-doubt
resentment
anger
futility
fills my heart
blackens my soul
I know I didn't take
the easiest road
and sometimes
I wish I had
chosen differently
chosen something easier
that didn't make me question
constantly
I feel a sense of angst
of restlessness
a hunger in my soul
for something more
than this humdrum life
I hate being a housewife
I'm not any good at it
wash the dishes
clean the floor

---

1. https://unsplash.com/@mxsh?utm_source=medium&utm_medium=referral

2. https://unsplash.com/?utm_source=medium&utm_medium=referral

scrub scrub scrub
then do it all again
after the kids swirl through
like a tornado
I am supposed to be a writer
a poet, an author, a blogger
and I write every day
but I have imposter syndrome
I feel like not enough
I feel like a failure
when my books don't sell
for another day in a row
Looking around my house
looking around my life
and everything it seems
has gotten so small
this microcosm
of what could be
no possibilities
only these four walls
holding me inside
This was supposed to be
an adventure
a new life
travel
fun
freedom
But instead it constrains
it holds me inside
it makes me less
it makes me small
I didn't come here

to put myself in a box
didn't leave my life behind
to give up my all
Before I had freedom
places to roam
Before I had sunshine
and a place of my own
I felt less lost
when I was working
and I feel lost now
without a sense
of purpose
I was supposed
to be a writer
so I type out these words
again for another day
into the ethers
of the interwebs
A poem about sadness
a poem about futility
How do I become more
How do I become who
I am supposed to be
here in this new place
cause goddess knows
I wasn't supposed
to be just a housewife

Self-love Inspires Us

Photo byTirza van Dijk[1] on Unsplash[2]
When you love yourself
it inspires you
to be your best self
and to love others more
When your cup is running
to overflowing with joy
all that joy
overflows to others
The happier you are
your happiness shines
outward from your smile
like a blinding light
into a dark world
When you love yourself
it helps you
and those around you
because you become your best
and inspire others
to be their best too
Love is a dance
love is joy
love is freedom
The more you love

1. https://unsplash.com/@tirzavandijk?utm_source=medium&utm_medium=referral

2. https://unsplash.com/?utm_source=medium&utm_medium=referral

the more love spreads
out from your hands
in kind acts to others
Love yourself
love those around you
love everyone more
and that love
pays it forward
Love only creates
more love
it flows
it blossoms
it becomes infectious
like the laughter
of a small child
Love asks for nothing
love gives
love takes for nothing
love lives
Hidden inside our heart
but pouring out
through our hands
through our smiles
through our acts
of charity
Love is beauty
love is kindness
love is gentleness
love is wisdom
Love is the heart
of all things meaningful

Shattered Dreams

Image by Thomas[1] from Pixabay[2]
I just want
the pain to stop
this wretched
endless sadness
that shrouds
everything in blackness
I tried to be happy
I tried to shine
to make a difference
and make things
a little easier
for someone somewhere
suffering just like me
I don't know how
to go on
I just stagger
a few steps forward
and then I fall
Lying on the ground
looking up

1. https://pixabay.com/users/didgeman-153208/?utm_source=link-attribution&utm_medium=referral&utm_campaign=image&utm_content=480367
2. https://pixabay.com/?utm_source=link-attribution&utm_medium=referral&utm_campaign=image&utm_content=480367

at the inky blackness
the moonless sky
the cold ground beneath
the rain pours down
hitting my face
It doesn't matter
what I do
what I need
what I want
nothing changes
nothing ever gets
any easier
Each step as though
with weighted feet
slogs softly forward
dragging limbs
stumbling blindly
through the forests
of endless emptiness
Tripping now and again
over rocks and trees
stepping in puddles
soaked to the skin
feeling the coldness
like that of death
though I yet live
Shadows
of my former self
slip through this
waking nightmare
the piece of myself
that used to be

alive
the me that used to have
a shred of hope
that refused to die
well it died
and nothing is left
Just darkness
and empty days
wishing to hide
my face from the sun
wishing to scream
through this charred
and blackened throat
swelled shut
I want to cry
I want to run
I want to sleep
so I don't feel
love hate love
it spirals
back to so much pain
I cannot live
or dream again

Shrouded in Mystery

Photo byIlona Panych[1] on Unsplash[2]
No matter how certain
we think the future is
life is always a bit
shrouded in mystery
No plans are without
circumstances that change
nothing set in stone
that can't be unwritten
no matter how much
we think or we try
to make sense
of the way things go
We meet by chance
strangers in the street
faces unknown
become much loved
and change our lives
Every day is a chance
an opportunity
for something more
to change our fate
by simple chance
Things go forward

1. https://unsplash.com/@we_are_details?utm_source=medium&utm_medium=referral

2. https://unsplash.com/?utm_source=medium&utm_medium=referral

and sometimes
circle back
to where we start
all over again
Older and sometimes
wiser or only
more jaded and bitter
sad from truths
that reveal themselves
in ways we never thought
Other times though
life shines so bright
it reveals things better
than we dreamed possible
and life unravels
in ways it never seemed
Everything we touch
everything we dream
is like moonbeams
gliding by in front of us
carried by the wind
Starshine above
green grass below
wind through the trees
whispers in the night
beckoning us forward
further into the unknown

Sit With Your Broken Heart for a While

Photo byMarah Bashir[1] on Unsplash[2]
Sit with your broken heart
in your hands for a while
turn it over and over
and see where it cracks
Like a rubix cube
it seems hard to solve
sometimes impossible
but nothing
is really impossible
You can fix it
if you turn it over enough
you can find a solution
though it may not be easy
Love isn't enough to fix us
it is often the thing
that broke us
in the first place
A love that takes us
far away from home
love that asks for sacrifice
and leaves us all alone
Love is the breaking
of everything we know

1. https://unsplash.com/@marahbashir?utm_source=medium&utm_medium=referral

2. https://unsplash.com/?utm_source=medium&utm_medium=referral

it takes us on a path
that strips us naked
and leads us
through the fires
of the dark night
of the soul
When we love too much
when we need too much
it wounds our hearts
and tears us up inside
Depending on love
is childlike and foolish
because love isn't enough
to sustain our hearts
We need to find ourselves
not depend on someone else
to complete us inside
When we search for love
we are often incomplete
looking for another half
to make us whole
But when two halves come together
they forget they are supposed
to grow into a whole
each one on their own
instead of staying half
to be a single whole
I can't be a half anymore
I am more like two thirds
and your half
doesn't fit anymore
it chafes at me

and doesn't let me grow
How do I help you grow too
so you become a whole
on your own
and I a whole too
and we can be more
than just two halves
always feeling incomplete
Love will always wound us
when we see ourselves as half
we allow a love that is partial
a love that is conditional
that doesn't accept us
as we learn to grow
How do we find ourselves
how do we love ourselves
and learn to be a whole
First we have to break
first we have to bend
we need to learn
to shift with the wind
go our way alone
for a time
then come back together
both whole and stronger

Surrender to the Self

Photo byKhamkéo Vilaysing[1] on Unsplash[2]
Surrender to the Self
to the Spirit
to the oneness
that is all that is
Surrender your thoughts
surrender your heart
surrender your feelings
surrender your faith
Become a part of that oneness
become more open inside
shed all the layers of
all the things
that aren't really you
Step out of the dream
of what you thought
life was
and into the beauty
and abundance
of the life of the soul
You are Spirit
you are Soul
you are oneness
You are the watcher

1. https://unsplash.com/@mahkeo?utm_source=medium&utm_medium=referral

2. https://unsplash.com/?utm_source=medium&utm_medium=referral

of your thoughts
you are the mirror
that you see yourself in
Reflected and reflecting
you are both and
neither one at once
You are the essence
of time and the universe
condensed into a form
that lives here on earth
your feet grazing the sand
at the edge
of the great ocean
You stare at that ocean
so vast and sleepless
the waves crashing
again and again
against the shore
You are like that ocean
you are like the tide
and the moon that brings
the tide to the shore
Vast and sleepless mother
home where we still slumber
in this dreamland
all the things that still
we have yet to understand
They are there
in the blink of an eye
all the things we see
all the things we try
All the truths hidden

right there in plain sight
all the things we don't notice
as our souls forget to take flight
All knowledge is here
at our fingertips
all compassion is there
in the space of our hearts
and all wisdom
is inside our own souls
We know the truth
we see the truth
we speak the truth
we are the truth
Revealed by the Self
to the self
through the self
And we can soar
to great heights
sail ships
to the farthest shore
we can find all the wisdom
that the world has in store
We are all and we
are beautiful
we are the boundless Self
we are the Soul

The Beauty of Allowing

Photo byLina Trochez[1] on Unsplash[2]

There is beauty
in allowing life to unfold
in the way that it wants to
and there is beauty
in trusting the universe
to take us the right way
that we are meant to go
We take twists and turns
through forests and streams
twisting like sunshine
in riddles and dreams
everywhere we go
is where we are supposed
to be
It is time now
to make life beautiful
to embrace its fullness
with a sense of wonder
and openness
a sense of joy and freedom
We know not where
life's roads may take us
and we journey on

---

1. https://unsplash.com/@lmtrochezz?utm_source=medium&utm_medium=referral

2. https://unsplash.com/?utm_source=medium&utm_medium=referral

through space and time
in a dance of beauty
with rhythm and rhyme
Going ever forward
onward and upward
twisting and turning
like leaves on the wind
swirling with colors
like flowers and rainbows
Flowing like a river
or a stream to the ocean
we know the destination
but not the journey
we all dissolve
into endless oneness
but before that
we journey onward
Together for a moment
in our separation
we walk these paths
before we go back
home to being starlight

The Death of Us

A poem
How do you mourn something
you never really had
why does it feel like death inside
and why am I so sad?
You always enjoyed
being the life of the party
while I was just waiting
for the guests to leave
so I could be alone
with you
Eventually even the times
at the end of the night
would never really come
you didn't hold me in your arms
anymore
we didn't fall asleep together
busy being parents
and trading childcare
I just became
a babysitter and
another pair of hands
to lighten your load
but what about my load
and all the things
I carried alone?
The times you loved me

grew fewer and
further between
until I began to wonder
if they would come
again at all
Something else
was always more important
something else
always needed to be done
You were right there
but always out of reach
staring into the screen
to unwind from the day
You were right there
in body only
and your mind and heart
a thousand miles away
I shouldn't have to beg
for you to love me
I shouldn't have to beg
for you to care
I shouldn't go to sleep
and cry that you aren't there
Every day the pain
grows a little stronger
every day my heart breaks
when I wait
a little longer
Longer for you to come home
to ask about the day
to dream about tomorrow
and wonder if

I should even stay
How can we build
a future together
when we never are
really together anymore
It's been a long time now
since you caressed my skin
held me a little closer
asked how I have been
Every day is dark and silent
and my tears can fall in peace
mourning for our lost love
and begging for release

The Quest for Freedom

Photo byFuu J[1] on Unsplash[2]
We think ourselves chained
by all our responsibilities
that we do day by day
we have a routine
we have structure
but the truth is
at any moment
we can break free
we just have to decide
We have to decide
that we are free
We can always do
whatever we want
we just have to
remember and see it
feel it in our bones
go free and run
feel the sand in our toes
on a beach somewhere
beside the great ocean
The ocean has always been there
beckoning us to come home
to those crashing waves

---

1. https://unsplash.com/@fuuj?utm_source=medium&utm_medium=referral
2. https://unsplash.com/?utm_source=medium&utm_medium=referral

the touch of the sand and
the caress of the sea
the feel of the sun
on your face and
the wind in your hair
Run free along the sand
splash in tide pools
return to yourself
return to your great mother
the sea

The Quest for Meaning

Photo byWonderlane[1] on Unsplash[2]
We journey onward
through the night
searching forward
for a ray of light
to beckon us forward
out of this tunnel
that seems endless
Always searching it seems
but what we find isn't
always what we
were looking for
And we journey
always forward
looking to the horizon
for a glimpse of the sun
will it rise soon
and break the darkness
of this endless night
Breathing in the stillness
no fright in this darkness
only resignation
to leave the past behind
somewhere in this night

---

1. https://unsplash.com/@wonderlane?utm_source=medium&utm_medium=referral

2. https://unsplash.com/?utm_source=medium&utm_medium=referral

and wake to the new dawn
transformed like a butterfly
unwrapped from a cocoon
What are these silken threads
that hold me in place
as I grow and change
and gain these wings
there is pain
in the transformation
Leaving my comfort zone
far behind
and going forward
into the unknown
of a different life
a different me
as I arrive somewhere
transformed
into a strange creature
one who can fly
I don't know how to fly
all I did before was crawl
but that life
is behind me now and
this new life opens up
as I wake from this slumber
and shed the silken strings
that held me in place
now I can move again
at a faster pace
through the air this time
Life takes us new directions
it gives us new realizations

it transforms our mindset
and makes us over new
We can't go back to what was
for we are not the same
as we were even yesterday
we have transformed
into something new
and a new life awaits
full of new dreams
new faces and new things
for us to see, do and be

The Stuff Our Souls are Made Of

Image byJörg Prieser[1] from Pixabay[2]
Our souls are born from stardust
a brightness borh
as stars collide
expanding
and contracting universe
of endless, blinding night
We rise
we fall
we're going home
we know it all
Answers we seek
deep within ourselves
within the universe
and nature itself
The nature of one
is the nature of all
an end to duality
an end to suffering
The road long and winding
up the steepest hill

---

1. https://pixabay.com/users/joergip31-3593984/?utm_source=link-attribution&utm_medium=referral&utm_campaign=image&utm_content=4396489
2. https://pixabay.com/?utm_source=link-attribution&utm_medium=referral&utm_campaign=image&utm_content=4396489

but now
we flow back down
like water
melted from the icecaps
forming into a stream
flowing to the sea
that great, sleepless mother
from which we all came
Long ago
once upon a dream
we lived on a star
to fall with a scream
What is the nature
of all things beautiful
why do we prize
all the things that shine
We prefer light to darkness
but sometimes
we face a moonless night
shrouded in mists
without our faithful guide
to light our way home

The Things We Long For

©Tugores34[1] |Megapixl.com[2]

They say that longing
is older than love
by far
The things we long for
searching for an answer
a whisper in the night
Reaching above
towards the moon
and her bright light
We wish for ourselves
for the world itself
to find peace and patience
amidst the sands
in the hourglass
of sifting time
What are these things
we long for deep inside?
What answers do we seek
as we throw away our pride?
How do we grow stronger
like whispers in the wind
when we still don't understand
when we still so often falter

---

1. https://www.megapixl.com/tugores34-stock-images-videos-portfolio

2. https://www.megapixl.com/

Life is beauty and
life is pain
both intertwined
inseparably
Hearts broken
as we find our way
looking for deeper love
than that which we find
Knowing somehow
there is more out there
than what we have seen
Our eyes can't see
but the truth we find
deep in our hearts
unbroken
All the pain and
all the scars
you still remain
somehow hopeful
that there is still
more out there
for you to find
We think ourselves weak
as we long for love
but we are strong
as we are still seeking
through all the sadness
the tears and the pain
we keep going forward
Even if you stop
and cry for a while
eventually tears stop

and you rise
to journey onward

The Things You Want from Me

Photo byJacob Rank[1] on Unsplash[2]
The things you want from me
are always unfair
like I am living
as a side character
in other people's lives
instead of starring in mine
My life is not my life
my wants are not my wants
my needs are not my needs
my heart is not my own
all of them belong
to all of you
my family
Sometimes I wonder
if that is what being a woman is
to always support others
but no one supports you
Or has my identity
been stripped away
by the years
since I was young
and now others
my children

---

1. https://unsplash.com/@jacobaustinrank?utm_source=medium&utm_medium=referral

2. https://unsplash.com/?utm_source=medium&utm_medium=referral

carry the torch forward
Do we only live
when we are young?
Do our dreams die
long before our bodies
and our hearts decay
while housed within us
knowing that our lives
our dreams
will go always unfulfilled
Is it only anger
and resentment that stays
while everything else
silently fades away
making room for only
emptiness
A broken heart
a wasted life
years of experience
that take me here
but here
is nowhere
Not who I want to be
not where I want to be
not sure at this point
what that would look like
I put my dreams on hold
for you
But no one ever
did that for me
no one ever
cared enough

to put me first
Yeah, I am resentful
of this whole world
that conspired all my life
to make me small
Now I am so small
I am nothing at all
an empty shell
a fading husk
a broken doll
a face with lips
that move
but like the Tin Man
no heart inside
long ago it died
rotted and withered
disappeared away
and no one noticed
Now I am empty
left with only broken
promises and
empty dreams
shattered hopes
of what used to be
what was supposed to be
that never panned out
You tell me
the future is bright
ahead
but I can only look back
like Lot's wife
turned to a pillar of salt

stuck forever in place
here I rot

The Truth of the Soul

Photo byMohamed Nohassi[1] on Unsplash[2]
What is the truth of the soul?
what happens when we die?
what happens when we live?
We circle forward
circle back
birth, death, rebirth
And it isn't the moments
that we spend suspended
in the world beyone this
that is the mystery
it is this life and
the meaning in the madness
We shouldn't be asking
what happens when we die
we should be asking
why we live
What are we meant to do?
where are we meant to go?
who are we meant to be?
How do we become
the best of ourselves?
how do we make it count?
how do we creat meaning?

1. https://unsplash.com/@coopery?utm_source=medium&utm_medium=referral

2. https://unsplash.com/?utm_source=medium&utm_medium=referral

For me
it circles back to love
and the faces
of those near and dear
wanting their happiness
and to ease their fear
Mother of children
friend and lover
listener
We hear the souls of others
and the things they love
the things they fear
the things they want
to accomplish or do
How do we know
how to make it meaningful
do we have to be deep
and spiritual
or wild and free
do we create something
take walks in the woods
or play at the beach?
Playing like a child
dreaming like a mystic
writing like a poet
Art, life, love, music, friendship, dance
Is there a meaning to it all
or is it all just chance?

This isn't the Best Poem in the World

This is only a tribute

Photo byTrust "Tru" Katsande[1] on Unsplash[2]

I write sad little poems
that are echoes of feeling
whispered in the night
and today I read something
that reminded me why I write
I write to feel alive.
The feel of the pages under my hands
like the caress of a lover's hands
shrouded in darkness
the feel of a kiss
the taste of coffee and cigarettes
it's not PC to be a smoker anymore
but I don't care
I'm not good at being PC
I want to live an extraordinary life
I want to write something filled
with raw emotion
a tribute to all those
who have gone before
a tribute to my younger self
there in the coffee house
reading a poem about cutting

---

1. https://unsplash.com/@iamtru?utm_source=medium&utm_medium=referral

2. https://unsplash.com/?utm_source=medium&utm_medium=referral

to the sound of improv jazz
Not caring what anyone thinks
not caring what they say only
caring if I can make them feel
some kind of raw realness
I don't rhyme.
I am the Sylvia Plath
of the millennial generation
only when you stick your head
in an electric oven
nothing happens
Someone told me once
I write like her and I wonder
if he alluded to me dying like her
or if he knew that I
used to think about death
way to fucking frequently
back in those days
Now I am more pragmatic
more balanced
but there is still a fire
burning in my soul
still a longing
to become whole
Writing brings me that
it brings me love and life
and a new book is like
making love with someone beautiful
the words flying onto the page
and not a care in the world
I love my new lovers
I love my new poems

I love my new books
I love to write them
even if no one reads them
Write for an audience
they say
sometimes my audience
is an audience of one
it is a younger me
who doesn't know
the answers yet
who doesn't see
that there is still hope
and it isn't fleeting
as it feels like
when you are young

Thoughts Running Wild

©Jeanneprovost[1] |Megapixl.com[2]

Our thoughts
like wild horses running
in directions all their own
taking pathways
their reasons not shown
We take this way and that
we try to find our way
following one thought
then another
fleeting moments
when we are truly present
But most of the time
we aren't here
we are somewhere
far away
not looking
at what we see
Sometimes strange things
seep through our consciousness
like strange dreams
though we yet wake
and we follow them
aimlessly at times

1. https://www.megapixl.com/jeanneprovost-stock-images-videos-portfolio

2. https://www.megapixl.com/

this way and that
Trying to find our way
find our answers
to the meaning of life
and what we do next
Sometimes not the same
the path that we tread
and the path of our dreams
so far apart
our thoughts
and our actions
How do we reconcile
our deepest fears
and our deepest needs
to find the truth
of where we need to be

Tracing Circles in the Sand

Image byRajitha Tennakoon[1] from Pixabay[2]
Tracing circles in the sand
reminiscent of the brilliant mandalas
that the monks make
spending ages of time
to create something beautiful
that you know will wash away
©Zanskar[3] |Megapixl.com[4]
Creating beauty
that you know is fleeting
the same way that we know
our lives are fleeting
that all things
with time
are transient
A sense of purpose
we create
cities and towns
walls to hold

1. https://pixabay.com/users/rajitha2tpb-1137521/?utm_source=link-attribution&utm_medium=referral&utm_campaign=image&utm_content=883068
2. https://pixabay.com/?utm_source=link-attribution&utm_medium=referral&utm_campaign=image&utm_content=883068
3. **https://www.megapixl.com/zanskar-stock-images-videos-portfolio**
4. **https://www.megapixl.com/**

our lives inside
Yet with time
those too will fade
perhaps someday
our ancestors will life
in the shadows
of these steel cities
taking shelter
in remnants of the past
©Zzz1b[5] |Megapixl.com[6]
Perhaps we are foolish
to think the things
we build will last
Though I live in a house
today that was built
over a century ago
Things today
are temporary
and transient
Like so many grains of sand
traced in little circles
to be washed away
by the constancy
of the tides and the sea
Somethings really do
last forever
don't they?
The sand
the sun
the moon

---

5. https://www.megapixl.com/zzz1b-stock-images-videos-portfolio

6. https://www.megapixl.com/

the sea
the tides
But not you and me
no matter how we
may try to be remembered
the things we create
are frail and transient
these words uttered
silently into the ether
will someday
silently pass away
How do we know
what the future holds
with any sense
of consistency?
The idea that things last
is just an illusion
and soon just like that
our time too
will have passed

Trapped in Emptiness

Photo byKeith Hardy[1] on Unsplash[2]
Trapped in the emptiness
this void of time and space
that hovers before me
like a blank slate
taunting me
telling me that things
are never going to get better
only probably worse
My dreams will never
be fulfilled
it's time to give them up
time to let the wind
wash away
all the things I wanted
open my hands
and let it all go
How do you let go
of the life
you longed so badly
to have
to the dreams of home
and a family to love
What do you do when love

1. https://unsplash.com/@keithhardy2001?utm_source=medium&utm_medium=referral

2. https://unsplash.com/?utm_source=medium&utm_medium=referral

doesn't seem to be enough
and every word just cuts
like a knife to your heart
making things so much worse
All alone now with
my dark, spiraling thoughts
that tell me the future
is just a bleak and lonely mess
where I will walk alone always
through the desert
parched with a thirst
that can not be quenched
Looking for a path
looking for an answer
to make the pain stop
to make the darkness
fade from my sight
and let me see again
I feel obscured
shrouded in clouds
where none can see
my invisible pain
Heartbreak after heartbreak
telling me my choices
were completely wrong
my intentions impure
and what I wanted
isn't fulfilling at all
Letting my dreams die
like wilting flowers
watered for a while
but the stems have been cut

and they can't grow anymore
Life has lost its luster
and the shine has dulled
no sun, moon or stars
to light my path now
Where do I go
when everything
everywhere just
looks so empty

Twin Souls

Photo byBernard Hermant[1] on Unsplash[2]

Ours was never
a whirlwind romance
it was something
that moved quietly
in the silence of souls
and it made me feel
like I could be whole
I loved you from afar
though you were close
but just across
a crowded room
and we talked
late at night over drinks
when everyone had gone
You made me realize
that the past is gone
and you a part of that past
are also gone now
leaving me here alone
I remembered you
dreamed of you
before I met you
even your tattoo

1. https://unsplash.com/@bernardhermant?utm_source=medium&utm_medium=referral

2. https://unsplash.com/?utm_source=medium&utm_medium=referral

But I didn't know
how much you
loved someone else
before I met you
and that you would never
want to hold me close
it took time to
figure out
And when I did
I let you go
left you to grieve
what you had lost
and in doing so
I lost you too
Lost to time again
until our souls
live again
in the land of our birth
where we walked
those bright fields
in the tall grass
at the edge of the cliff
with those great white ships
sailing off in the distance
We lived another life
we dreamed another dream
and found ourselves here
on this other plane
But how do we reconcile
the dreams with the regret
and all the times I held you
were never enough

to make you love me
I wasn't what you wanted
and you only here
to show me a lesson
to lead me to another
who would love me fully
I wonder at so much
now that you are gone
I wonder why I miss you
and remember
our brief love affair
so deeply now
after time has gone by
So many years
we could have had
if you would have
loved me
But you didn't
maybe you couldn't
maybe we were both
too broken alone
and together
not good enough
to take away the pain
of all we had lost
before we found each other
I wonder my friend
what could have been
and I feel like
it is a betrayal
of what I have now
although you are gone

again to the great shore
with those white ships
Do you hear my voice there
do you feel my loneliness
do you hear my longing
feel my wondering
or do you see something else
now that you are gone
off to that other place
the place of our birth
Twins
Yet all these years apart
made us our own people
not so enmeshed together
the way we were then
when all we had
was each other
I lament for you now
I miss your sweet face
and I send this message
silently from my soul
to your soul
my bright angel
I hope you find peace
and healing
there in the otherworld

Unanswered Questions

Image bySusan Cipriano[1] from Pixabay[2]

I sit here now with
unanswered questions
shattered dreams
crushed beneath my
little bleeding feet
like shards of glass
they reflect back at me
the emptiness
of my fake smile
holding back the tears
that no one cares to see
waiting til I'm alone
until it's only me
And then I will cry again
let loose this flood
waiting til the lights are out
and the house is silent and dark
beneath the light of the moon
or a neon flashbulb light
then I will cry

1. https://pixabay.com/users/susan-lu4esm-7009216/?utm_source=link-attribution&utm_medium=referral&utm_campaign=image&utm_content=3394947
2. https://pixabay.com/?utm_source=link-attribution&utm_medium=referral&utm_campaign=image&utm_content=3394947

my silent, forgotten tears
How many years struggling
to be the best of myself
and still I can't break free
of all these hands
clutching needily at me
it's always something more
than the things I can give
always something else
that won't let me live
I want to break free
I want to dance and dream
somewhere under the stars
free from tears at last
but even after all this time
I just can't seem to find
an answer anywhere
Why are dreams so fragile
like whisps of smoke
beckoning us forward
then they disappear
when we are almost there
almost to the light
then things shatter
they always break
like baubles of glass
for the Christmas tree
rolling under the couch
I want to live a dream
but is it all a lie
when they told us
we could be anything

that we want to be
Do I need to stop wanting
anything at all
do I need to stop
answering their call
shut up you stupid dreams
stop making me believe
that there is something
better out there somewhere
because it isn't for me

Unfinished Stories

©Jrabelo[1] |Megapixl.com[2]
Sometimes the things
we choose to be in life
can be self-harming
and the relationships
with those we love
can be like drowning
in other people's
thoughts and feelings
We make our choices
from people pleasing
and don't choose
ourselves
often enough
to be really happy
The weight
of other's feelings
heavy on my shoulders
and I feel like
I am crumbling
I may not be
your first choice
but I am a good choice
and I deserve

---

1. https://www.megapixl.com/jrabelo-stock-images-videos-portfolio

2. https://www.megapixl.com/

to be chosen
How do we choose people
who won't choose us back?
Life feels like circles
going in wrong directions
of same-direction turns
left-left-left
right-right-right
right back to where
I started from
and feeling foolish
How do I keep coming back
to the same people and places
how do I break free
from all these blank faces
staring back at me
like nothing has changed
only me
only inside
I know things now
that I didn't know then
but still I circle back
again and again
to these same lessons
still not learned
If I want someone else
to choose me
I have to choose myself
first

Unsure

Photo bymarianne bos[1] on Unsplash[2]
Unsure of where to go
unsure where to call my home
where am I going to go
where am I going to roam?
How do you move forward
when you are stuck in place
decision on the horizon
but still out of reach
Waiting for the future
to start
waiting for my new life
to begin
Where do you go
when you are waiting
and walking in circles
not ready for a change
but looking for a chance
to make things right
Staying stuck
staying frozen
feet glued to the floor
trying to get away
and get out the door

1. https://unsplash.com/@mariannebos?utm_source=medium&utm_medium=referral

2. https://unsplash.com/?utm_source=medium&utm_medium=referral

Waiting for the Tears to Come

©Starush[1] |Megapixl.com[2]

Sometimes my whole life
feels tied up to loneliness
there is a space inside my heart
that has always been empty
that has always felt broken
ever since I can remember
I always felt cold
like I was left out in the rain
for far too long
There are scars that don't heal
and time doesn't ease
the pain away
There is no balm
to ease this endless ache
that I don't know where
it even came from
Always I felt alone
always I felt sad
hopeless and broken
even when I was young
Was I ever young?
I see it like pictures
taken in freeze frame

---

1. https://www.megapixl.com/starush-stock-images-videos-portfolio

2. https://www.megapixl.com/

like a window
into another time
someone else's life
never mine
I stand there faded
far in the background
of smiling happy faces
like a bad photo bomb
Tears I tried to hide
in the silence of the night
for so many years now
they come in the daylight
I can't stop it anymore
I tried to be my best
I tried to find love
I tried to be enough
but it just never was
So much that I regret
so much that I pretend
but you can't try to fake
your way through everything
with a smile on your face
eventually
the smile comes off
Faded like pieces
of tattered lace
a shattered tiara
a broken vase
thrown away
in a landfill somewhere
only taking up space
Eyes don't see me now

they can't find my face
hidden in my hands
sobbing red
How do you erase
the words that cut
deeper than a knife
how do you forgive
how do you forget
and let it go
Why is it always me
who has to change
who has to forgive
why am I always
the one at fault
No matter which relationship
I gave it my all but still
you had to feel like
you could make me small
not enough
for you to really love
I wanted love so badly
this empty shell
of the invisible child
never held in loving arms
I was like an orphan
held at arms length
or left in bed to cry
Why couldn't you love me
no matter how hard I try?
Maybe love isn't about trying
maybe it's about letting to
and opening yourself up

to be something more

Waves on the Sand

photo owned by author
Life passes us by
like waves on the sand
coming back and yet
never the same again
a state of constant change
a feeling of lack
the contentment of serenity
We spend time
passing between moments
that stick in our memories
walking back and forth
to and fro
not always looking
at where we go
Moments between moments
time spent waiting
always goes slowly
and when we are living
in the thick of things
time passes quickly
and feels like it is never enough
to make us feel satisfied
Moments between moments
when we should be living
instead of waiting
for something else to come

those big moments
aren't the only ones
that we have
there are others
every day
that we let pass by
without participating
though they seem
to flow by slowly
How do we grab ahold
of each moment fully
like time standing still
like a dance we glide
making the most
of each and every step
that we take on this Earth
Not knowing if this step
will be the last we dance
never really sure
if we have another chance
to do the things we want to
instead of things we have to
So much of life
we are barely surviving
much less living
not participating
in the dance of life
letting it fly by
on the wings of time lost
waiting for something
better or something more
we let things pass by

How do we take better advantage
of the things we love
while we have them
How do we waste less time
on simply waiting
to do something else
Grab life
embrace it fully
take advantage
of each and every day
They say build a life
that you don't need
a vacation from
I think that it's true
you should have some life
in every day instead
of only surviving
in the space between moments

We are All Alone

©Lariotus[1] |Megapixl.com[2]
Lonely, lonely, lonely
I have walked through hell
and now I'm walking back
the devil wouldn't take me
even he couldn't stand
to see the pain in my eyes
couldn't sit with me
and add any torture
to what I feel inside
so tortured already
by silent screams in the night
Too tired to keep going
too tired to try to fight
for myself any longer
so I just walk unseen
through these streets
alone in the night
alone in the day
people don't say hello
and just pass by
on their way so quickly
Ever we walk alone
all of us enshrouded

1. https://www.megapixl.com/lariotus-stock-images-videos-portfolio
2. https://www.megapixl.com/

in our own thoughts
feelings and emotions
held tightly inside
in this delicate shell
afraid of breaking open
of being exposed in truth
to the light of the day
we are afraid to speak
so we go silently on
Truth is like the sun
it shines so brightly sometimes
then everything fades to dark
again silencing our souls
and giving birth to fear
of things untold
When we tell in confidence
we fear our truth will spread
on the winds of ignorance and indifference
or hate and judgement
in the faces of others
in their halting speech
when they try to reply
to secrets of hearts given
only to receive disgust
We try to be open for a while
but after a time we shut down
tired of trying to be heard
and have our words felt
by another heart than ours
People want to cling
to one another tightly
afraid of letting go

of someone we love
but only halfway know
We keep secrets even
from those closest to us
for those we fear the most
to have them judge us
and be found wanting
Love kept at arms length
is barely love at all
it is like being underwater
and breathing through a straw
about to sink as we swim
through these darkened waters
yet on we go afraid
of drowning farther still

We are All Fragile

Photo byDominik Scythe[1] on Unsplash[2]

I am thin and fragile
like a leaf on the wind
floating to and fro
which ever way
the wind may blow
A battered heart
a face with scars
inside I bleed
from years
that don't pass
gently
We are all fragile
hearts and souls
made as if
of gossamer fabric
beautiful when new
but easily torn
The years are not kind
nor are all the people
that come into our lives
Everyone tries
their best to be kind
but inside

1. https://unsplash.com/@drscythe?utm_source=medium&utm_medium=referral

2. https://unsplash.com/?utm_source=medium&utm_medium=referral

we are often selfish
guarding our hearts
but not the other
hearts that are given
into our keeping
We are all fragile
and easily torn
we begin to break
the day we are born
We all break easily
without learning
how to bend
time takes its toll
and we wonder
how it will end

We are All Grains of Sand

Photo byfrank mckenna[1] on Unsplash[2]

Our lives are small
like grains of sand
broken from rocks
ground down by the sea
Time passes
and one great rock
becomes many
small grains of sand
We pass through the hourglass
waiting for our time to come
Waiting for the day
that this great sea
will take us home
to the place
of our birth
We come from stardust
and to stardust
someday we return
So small
so insignificant
and yet it feels like
our lives are so big
But look down on the Earth

1. https://unsplash.com/@frankiefoto?utm_source=medium&utm_medium=referral

2. https://unsplash.com/?utm_source=medium&utm_medium=referral

from outer space and
we are smaller than ants
our world of blue and green
showing only the sea
and mountain ranges
not even our houses
much less ourselves
We think ourselves
more important
than we are
in the scheme of things
We think our problems
and our woes greater
than perspective shows
they actually are
We are small
tiny
like ants
or stardust
or grains of sand

We Get By More Than We Overcome

Image byStockSnap[1] from Pixabay[2]
We are the fallen
who have gotten back up
sometimes in the middle
of our story they call us
overcomers
thinking we have
made it through
But the path continues
and it is never easy
it draws us forward
beckoning us on
into the dawn
of a new day
Sometimes that day
is bright and beautiful
other times
we wake in terror
from dreams
that haunt us
into the daylight

---

1. https://pixabay.com/users/stocksnap-894430/?utm_source=link-attribution&utm_medium=referral&utm_campaign=image&utm_content=2605274
2. https://pixabay.com/?utm_source=link-attribution&utm_medium=referral&utm_campaign=image&utm_content=2605274

Life isn't always kind
sometimes we suffer
more than we deserve
No one deserves to suffer
and yet we all do
all too often
at each other's hands
The truth is not kind
And you've said, neither am I
— Toad the Wet Sprocket
We are often
each other's demons
The words we say
are the scars
we must recover from
later in life
or later today
Relationships crumble
like sand around us
sometimes leaving us
in ruin
Our own minds become
a shambles
and we stumble on in pain
I am not an overcomer
though it is true that once
I overcame the pain
But pain comes anew
with the dawn of a new day
and the face of one once loved
now has gone astray
No matter how much we love

no matter how much we strive
to live our best lives it happens
not all at once but
in an unfolding
that we change with time
Sometimes we become wise
sometimes sad
sometimes better
sometimes bad
Nothing is forever
and healing doesn't last
we pass again into madness
and for air we gasp
It is like swimming
with the current
that is ever changing
racing away so fast
Sometimes the river
reaches a calm place
and we can rest
we recharge
we feel as though
we have conquered
the rapids forever
Until new rapids come
dragging us under
the black water
once again

What do we Believe in?

Image byFractals99[1] from Pixabay[2]
What do we believe in
when behind the lies
there is nothing left
to be said or felt or done
in the name of light
and life
How do you move forward
when what you think
isn't what's right
How do you know the truth
when in the darkness it hides
elusive in the night
like a moonbeam
or a whisper of fate
Do we need the truth
or is finding
a convincing lie
enough to live on
as we go forward
trying not to stay stuck

---

1. https://pixabay.com/users/fractals99-779764/?utm_source=link-attribution&utm_medium=referral&utm_campaign=image&utm_content=2835909
2. https://pixabay.com/?utm_source=link-attribution&utm_medium=referral&utm_campaign=image&utm_content=2835909

Something lost inside myself
a missing piece
I can't seem to grasp
like an answer is hiding
on the other side
of a mirror
at the edges
of my vision
caught in glimpses
I turn to see what lies there
and in turning
it is gone
like so many whisps
of gentle breeze
we wonder now
like the wind blows
through the trees
Where is the truth hiding
where are the memories
of the things I have seen
all of the answers
shrouded in a dream
like a shadow of a shadow
a fragment of a whisper
a mystery of fate
There is so much hope
but it seems so thin
looking for peace
amid the silent screams
a broken heart bleeding
tired feet from walking
in circles always

onward and upward
but so slowly
falling back down
Two steps forward
three steps back
like a circle
somehow we scream
muffled voices
mouths taped shut
heart torn open
and yet we dream
How do we know
if something can be done
some way to struggle forward
and find another light
another vision
another hope
to end the endless night

What Makes Your Heart Sing

Photo byVidar Nordli-Mathisen[1] on Unsplash[2]
What is it that makes your heart sing?
what makes you feel free?
what makes your soul dance?
what catches your mind on fire?
Those are the things that matter
the things that bring you aliveness
the moments inbetween
doing what you need to do
and you stop to live
You stop to dance
you stop to run free
watch the geese
flying in the tree
Day by day small moments
where we reconnect
with ourselves
with friends and loved ones
over coffee or drinks
and tell our stories
That is where we live
in the spaces of life like
filling this blank page
or a painter's canvas

---

1. https://unsplash.com/@vidarnm?utm_source=medium&utm_medium=referral

2. https://unsplash.com/?utm_source=medium&utm_medium=referral

or music in the air
That is our aliveness
that is our beauty
that is our shine
that is our brilliance
The ability to create something
like a bridge or a skyscraper
a rocket to the moon
a book or a poem
Life is tears
it is silence
the smile of a child
the rain on the glass
Things that make us feel
things that make us free
the bringing of joy
or the brokenness of pain
all make us feel alive
in those small moments
That's what life is
a series of small moments
like still-frame photography
or one of those flip books
or an old-time movie
still frames
moving through time

Where is the Wind Blowing?

Photo byOliver Hihn[1] on Unsplash[2]
Where is the wind blowing me
bidding me to go
out into the unknown
but not knowing where
I am going to land
It is time to go
I can't stay here
but do I just let go
and let myself fly
on the wings of the wind
beating this way and that
How do I leave here
how do I release
all the expectations
and pains of the past
release everything
and fly like a balloon
up into the sky
Let go of the string
watch the colored ball go
flying away somewhere
and trusting its path
as it flies on the wind

1. https://unsplash.com/@mr_kuchen?utm_source=medium&utm_medium=referral

2. https://unsplash.com/?utm_source=medium&utm_medium=referral

carried somewhere new
How do we know that new
is going to be better
than what we leave behind
Seeds fly on the wind
to take root in new soil
so too
must our souls fly
in order to grow
in a place that is new
Trust in the process
and in spring growth
let the wind take you
so that you can start anew

Whispers and Dreams

Photo byNEOM[1] on Unsplash[2]

From somewhere
across the desolate plain
comes a whisper
begging you to come forward
to dream your dream again
Don't give up hope
it whispers
just a little farther
there is water waiting for you
a place to hang your hat
You stagger onward
watching tumbleweeds
twirling past you
through the dry creek beds
wondering how
much farther you can go
before you too
are dried and cracked
just tumbling
But ahead you see
at the foot of the mountains
a stream
that faint glint of blue

1. https://unsplash.com/@neom?utm_source=medium&utm_medium=referral

2. https://unsplash.com/?utm_source=medium&utm_medium=referral

against a lush green
you have arrived
After walking so long
with no hope in sight
you have found the trees
you have found something *alive*
after your endless wandering
You had no idea
if you wandered
without any hope
yet still you came
every tiny step forward
as those steps
became smaller
more frail
close to falling
you came on
And here you are
you have arrived
somewhere alive still
after all your searching
You put your face to the stream
tasting the clear, cool water
letting it rush past
your parched lips
cooling your sundried face
you pull your head back
looking up to the sky
you let out a laugh
You have arrived
it was worth it
you survived

Why do I Still Care?

Photo bytabitha turner[1] on Unsplash[2]
Why do I still care
in a world that has tried
to crush
all hope out of me
all these years
Why do I still hope
that the world
could be a good place
that everyone could
be happy
Why do I still believe
in inclusivity
in a world
so full of hate
Why do I still dream
of a place beyond the stars
where people live free
Do we have to wait
for the next lifetime
for things to change
Do we go into
the great beyond
somewhere

1. https://unsplash.com/@tabithabrooke?utm_source=medium&utm_medium=referral

2. https://unsplash.com/?utm_source=medium&utm_medium=referral

After we die
do we find peace
In this life
can we find enlightenment
How do we create hope
how do we create peace
when people don't seem
to want those things
No wonder there is
an epidemic of depression
and suicide
is a leading cause of death
people have given up
their hope has been crushed
by an uncaring world
So why do I still want
to be a beacon of hope
for people who are drowning
why do I still want to save them
with this tiny little boat
As long as one person
still cares
is that enough for hope
to live on in my heart
I guess it has to be
because I don't know how
to kill the hope inside me
as much as sometimes
I want to
Not caring
would be so much easier
than this pain

of caring so much
Would that I could sink
below the black waters
of ignorance and apathy
and stop feeling the pain
that caring brings
But if 40 years
of being in pain
couldn't crush this hope
then perhaps nothing can
I am cursed with caring
in an uncaring world
every day I feel the pain
and keep stumbling forward
going another step on
Not stopping
not giving up
For me giving up hope
would be akin to dying
why keep on living
if you don't care
I keep going
because I'm alive
I keep caring
because I exist
Without hope
without caring
there is only
endless blackness
and I can't resign
myself to that

Words I can't Say

Photo byengin akyurt[1] on Unsplash[2]
Words in my heart
spilling onto the page
things in my mind
that I just cannot say
and it hurts
What do you do
when you can't say everything
can't say anything
that matters most
and you don't know
who to talk to
Fear of being judged
fear of being not enough
of being too much
of telling secrets
that aren't mine to tell
And sometimes I feel
like I am trapped
in this world of silence
and here I am — a writer
how do I keep the words in?
How do I pretend
my feelings don't exist

---

1. https://unsplash.com/@enginakyurt?utm_source=medium&utm_medium=referral

2. https://unsplash.com/?utm_source=medium&utm_medium=referral

when they are spilling out
at the edges of my eyes
these tears uncried
the words unspoken
and I wonder when
the curse will be broken
that keeps me silent
How do I keep going
when I feel so broken
inside and sad
barely holding on
in so many ways
and how do I know
what will be enough
to ease the pain
Every day I feel
so much shame
at choices unmade
and things that I dream
things that I wish for
in the silence
of the night
How do I take the wrongs
and make them right?
So many secrets
mine and yours
and no words
to speak between us
How do we make it right?
I don't know what to say
don't know what to do
and it reminds me of that song

from back in the 90's
Don't speak
I know what you're thinking
and I don't need your reasons
don't tell me cause it hurts

You Ruined My Life

Photo byVince Fleming[1] on Unsplash[2]

You ruined my life
yes you
that face
in the mirror
the face of the one
who took it all away
piece by piece
brick by brick
everything
I had built
ruined
in one fell swoop
You ruined my life
you stupid girl
you made bad choices
that can't be unmade
You can't take back
the pain that you caused
to me and to others
dragging me down
to the depths of despair
Wallowing in self-pity
and self-blame

---

1. https://unsplash.com/@vincefleming?utm_source=medium&utm_medium=referral

2. https://unsplash.com/?utm_source=medium&utm_medium=referral

for letting things
get like this
get so bad that
I don't think this time
I can bounce back
You ruined my life
you stupid girl
with your willful
ignorance and arrogance
you thought you could
have it all
but you lost it all
instead
You couldn't settle
for 'good enough'
no.
You had to have better
you had to have more
you had to keep dreaming
and reaching higher
and higher still
until you fell
Broken legs
broken spine
you fell from
such a height
The paramedics now
just staring at you
and your stupid choices
knowing even they
can't fix you
back at the hospital

There is no miracle cure
for being stupid
and making bad choices
but there should be
there should be a way
to fix a hopeless situation
but that's why they call it
hopeless
All hope has gone
all reason flown
all sanity
gone to the winds
Stupid, stupid girl
you ruined it all

Don't miss out!

Visit the website below and you can sign up to receive emails whenever Nicole Dake publishes a new book. There's no charge and no obligation.

https://books2read.com/r/B-A-RYPWC-WRCMF

BOOKS 2 READ

Connecting independent readers to independent writers.

About the Author

Nicole Dake is a blogger, author, and mom of two. Nicole blogs about parenting with a focus on health & wellness for moms and kids. Nicole has a BA in Psychology with a minor in Religious Studies from University of Colorado, Paralegal Certification from Boston University.

Nicole is also a Spiritual Life Coach and ordained minister of the Universal Life Church Monastery.

Visit my blog at: https://medium.com/@nicoledake

Read more at https://medium.com/@nicoledake.

www.ingramcontent.com/pod-product-compliance
Lightning Source LLC
LaVergne TN
LVHW041019150826
845672LV00001B/135

* 9 7 9 8 2 2 7 6 7 9 0 3 1 *